Praise for *The Income Factory*

The Income Factory shows that by shifting their focus from the fickle market's ups and downs to the power of reinvesting and compounding income, investors can build their wealth abundantly while also sleeping well at night.
>—MARTIN FRIDSON, CFA, Publisher, *Forbes/Fridson Income Securities Investor*

A preeminent thought-leader in strategic income investing, Steve Bavaria inspires investors to break free of the financial industry's obsession with market price and to focus on what really matters: growing an income stream. A refreshing and practical good read for all, *The Income Factory* empowers us to invest in the right assets, for the right reasons, and with the right strategy.
>—KATHLEEN A. CORBET, Founder and Principal of Cross Ridge Capital, LLC

Steve is a visionary thinker who left his mark on Wall Street by creating a whole new category of credit ratings that helped transform the once sleepy leveraged loan market into a $1.3 trillion behemoth. *The Income Factory* is a must-read for investors who are looking to confidently generate investment income in today's yield-starved world.
>—STEVEN MILLER, Head of Leveraged Finance Intelligence at Fitch Solutions

Steven Bavaria's *Income Factory* is a simple yet elegant approach for the average investor to leverage the magnificent power of compound interest—Albert Einstein's eighth Wonder of the World. "He who understands it, earns it!"
>—"STANFORD CHEMIST," Founder and Publisher of CEF/ETF Income Laboratory on Seeking Alpha

Generating income from investment cash flows is an ancient concept, but it takes Steve Bavaria's unique blend of market and journalistic experience to reimagine it. With wonderful clarity and logic, *The Income Factory* challenges market value convention, offering the "non-heroic" benefits of credit payment streams. A must-read in a volatile and uncertain investing world.
>—RANDY SCHWIMMER, Head of Origination and Markets, Churchill Asset Management and Founder/Publisher, *The Lead Left*

Bavaria's "plain talk" on credit investing empowers investors to produce high-yield returns that are much easier to forecast than stock market moves.
—DIANE VAZZA, former Global Head of Fixed Income
Research at Standard & Poor's

Steve Bavaria's *The Income Factory* explains how high-yield investments can be used to achieve stock-market returns as good or better than the usual price-focused strategies. Cash returns are more reliable than market price returns and can be reinvested to create your own growth by buying more assets. Steve's plain-English explanations are a pleasure to read and easy to follow.
—DAVID VAN KNAPP, popular Seeking Alpha writer and author
of eight e-books on Dividend Growth Investing

The Income Factory takes the historical perspective of Benjamin Graham, equating free cash flow to current distributions, with a goal of growing cash flow dramatically over time. When you focus on what the portfolio produces versus paper gains/losses, you see the benefits of this "river of cash" to meet return goals rather than increased prices alone. A simple yet profound way to build portfolios that can increase cash flow even in bear markets, while helping avoid panic selling. I hope EVERY investor takes the time to read and follow this book's principles.
—JOHN COLE SCOTT, CFS, Chief Investment Officer at
CEF Advisors, Founder of CEFData.com

Steve Bavaria's *The Income Factory* describes how using high current cash yields to "create your own growth" through reinvestment and compounding is a more predictable way to build wealth than relying on "wishing, waiting, and hoping" the market will do it for you. I have long admired Steve's straightforward ability to communicate. Read, enjoy, and prosper!
—KAREN VAN DE CASTLE, former Wall Street banker,
consultant, and educator

Your book is an absolute MUST-READ for non-investment professionals. You are thoughtful, methodical, and not unnecessarily technical in telling people how to make money in the long run! Whatever you charge for the book will be a bargain for those who buy it and use its commonsense approach to investing.
—RICHARD W. THALER, Jr., Managing Partner,
Lieutenant Island Partners

Here's what investors on *Seeking Alpha* have said about *The Income Factory*:

I have been following Steven since 2013. I consider myself quite fortunate to have discovered him and his Income Factory concept.
—cayecaulker

Love the philosophy and the results. Thank you.
—Malka

Steven has one of the best retirement solutions out there. Keep up the good work.
—TSampson

Have been following and mimicking the Income Factory for about 18 months; Love the results.
—glippmann

As a technology and business systems analyst I always strived to design solutions that were simple, user-friendly, and very effective! Steven Bavaria has done just that with his "Income Factory" investment philosophy and approach!
—Eric Telmer

I want to thank you for your work here. Your articles have really affected my thinking. I was especially struck by the image of just having to finish the race instead of win it. Anyway, thanks again.
—jklugmn

Great stuff!
—phuongle1985

Collect the cash, re-invest in closed-end funds, and the income continues to grow every month.
—yieldplay

Thanks for your continued sound strategy!
—mgh4814

Your investment philosophy makes enormous sense for most; your focus on income, irrespective of where indexes might be today or tomorrow or were yesterday offers simplicity and effectiveness. It also allows the investor to do what the vast majority never do, and that's buy when there's a sale going on. Thank you for your significant and continued contributions.
　　　　—du4sloop

You are on my very limited "must-read" list.
　　　　—Pinot44

Great article and great education piece; can't wait to read the book.
　　　　—Alpha Gen Capital

Not having to win the race . . . but just finish . . . is pretty much my strategy for everything now. Thanks, S Bavaria.
　　　　—RABrow

Excellent article. I enjoy your rather humble writing style along with the financial analysis.
　　　　—Christopher Smith

You hit the nail on the head and that's why I love reading your articles. It's the Income that matters more so than the paper value.
　　　　—timeveritt

I am a fan of your Income Factory investing and have moved about 95% of my investments to this approach. Thank you for all your work and investment ideas.
　　　　—cjstockpicker

A huge thank you for being the straight shooter that you are. You have inspired me to learn more . . . and can't wait to buy your book. Really look forward to reading every article that you post.
　　　　—Billfisher

THE
INCOME
FACTORY

An Investor's Guide to
Consistent Lifetime Returns

STEVEN BAVARIA

Mc
Graw
Hill

New York Chicago San Francisco Athens London Madrid
Mexico City Milan New Delhi Singapore Sydney Toronto

4 5 6 7 8 LBC 28 27 26 25 24

ISBN   978-1-260-45853-4
MHID   1-260-45853-9

e-ISBN   978-1-260-45854-1
e-MHID   1-260-45854-7

Library of Congress Cataloging-in-Publication Data

Names: Bavaria, Steven, author.
Title: The income factory : an investor's guide to consistent lifetime returns / Steven Bavaria.
Description: New York : McGraw-Hill Education, [2020] | Includes bibliographical references and index.
Identifiers: LCCN 2019037070 (print) | LCCN 2019037071 (ebook) | ISBN 9781260458534 (hardcover) | ISBN 9781260458541 (ebook)
Subjects: LCSH: Investments. | Portfolio management.
Classification: LCC HG4521 .B4237 2020 (print) | LCC HG4521 (ebook) | DDC 332.6—dc23
LC record available at https://lccn.loc.gov/2019037070
LC ebook record available at https://lccn.loc.gov/2019037071

McGraw-Hill Education books are available at special quantity discounts to use as premiums and sales promotions or for use in corporate training programs. To contact a representative, please visit the Contact Us pages at www.mhprofessional.com.

To Albert Bavaria (1917–2014)
and
Lorna Bavaria (1918–2010)

Together they exemplified the "greatest generation" in their dedication to family, country, and community

Contents

Acknowledgments vii

Introduction: Wealth Without the Drama. 1

1   How to Use This Book. 9

2   Why Do We Invest? What Makes Us Wealthy? 19

3   How Mr. Market Captures Value 29

4   Income Factory: The Math, the Risks, and the Choices . . 43

5   What Sort of Income Factory Is Right for You? 63

6   Building Our Factory 87

7   Income Factory Model Portfolios 107

8   "Stretching" for Yield 125

9   Variations on the Theme. 139

10   The Taxonomy of Risk and Reward 153

11   Bonds, Interest Rates, and Credit Risk. 165

12   Senior Loans (High-Yield Bonds with Benefits) 177

13   Virtual Banks (aka "CLOs") 187

14   From Benjamin Graham to the Income Factory 207

Appendix: Financial Innovation—A Case Study. 213

Index. 219

Acknowledgments

Whatever insight and "outside-the-box" thinking I bring to *The Income Factory* stems from my good fortune in having been exposed to a remarkable assortment of people and experiences during successive careers at Bank of Boston (BKB), *Investment Dealers' Digest (IDD)*, and Standard & Poor's (S&P).

Bank of Boston taught me about the credit and risk principles that underpin the Income Factory philosophy. I am grateful to my many mentors, superiors, friends, colleagues, and fellow BKB alumni, who gave me opportunities to learn about credit and risk around the world, and supported my early and later literary efforts. They include George Ricker, Frank Aldrich, Tom Fransioli, George Phalen, Whit Knapp, Barry Wendell, Tony Davies, Sue and Frank Wellington, Ken Ingram, Sharon McClew, Skip Vonckx, John Garrels, Richard Thaler, Ben Moyer, Margaret Causey, George Yurchyshyn, Sally Warren, Eric Butler, John Lewis, Monty Belanger, and many others. Thanks also to my friend Tom Walsh, one of Boston's finest lawyers, who taught me about the other side of credit—how to recover loans that have "gone south."

My stint at *IDD* allowed me to make friends and work with some marvelously talented people, especially Chris Donnelly, Tim Cross, Wes Goodman, and Michael Vachon. Together we learned a lot about finance and capital markets, as well as how to dig up a story and meet a deadline under pressure.

S&P allowed me to focus on credit from a new perspective, as we introduced ratings to the syndicated loan market, helping its evolution into a separate asset class. I am grateful to my S&P colleagues and friends, Sandy Bragg, Ken Pfeil, Karen Van de Castle, Ed Emmer, Kathleen Corbet, John McGowan, Sol Samson, Gail Hessol, Marc Bickman, Bill Chambers, Diane Vazza, Ruth Yang, Marc Auerbach, Evan Gunter, and many others, for their support and encouragement. Special thanks to Steve Miller, whose start-up venture to track and report on high-yield credit became the industry standard as well as the "hood ornament" for S&P's overall presence in the leveraged finance market.

The *Seeking Alpha (SA)* community of editors, writers, and readers has provided me the vehicle and audience for trying out the "radical" ideas about focusing on the cash rather than on paper profits and losses that shaped our *Income Factory* strategy. Thanks to SA's management for its support, to my many followers and readers for their feedback and encouragement, and to SA's other writers and contributors who are my unofficial "research team." Especially to my colleague "Stanford Chemist" and his CEF/ETF Income Laboratory team, as well as to fellow contributors David Van Knapp and John Cole Scott.

My editors at McGraw-Hill, Donya Dickerson and Noah Schwartzberg, have shown wholehearted support from day one, first by seeing the potential in this project and then providing me with invaluable insights into how to organize my investing philosophy into a compelling, readable format. I am grateful to them and to their colleagues, Nora Hennick and Amanda Muller, for helping make this book a reality.

Finally, I'd like to thank my family for their encouragement, love, and support: my sisters, MaryAnn and Susan (the original writer in the family); my children, Abbey, David, Brian, and Mark; daughters-in-law Cynthia and Amanda; and most important of all, my wife, Betsy. Without her love, humor, patience, and care, my life—as a writer, father, husband—would hardly resemble what it is today.

Introduction

Wealth Without the Drama

The message most investors receive constantly from their brokers, advisors, cable channels, and other business media is that success depends mostly on placing "winning bets" on the right securities. Then you have to follow their progress 24-7, always being alert to signs of trouble that may require you to bail out or change course at a moment's notice.

Whew! That's a lot to worry about. No wonder so many average investors are stressed out and confused, or throw up their hands and buy overpriced annuities and other heavily promoted products and services that promise to relieve them of the angst and insecurity of investing for their own futures.

While investing can indeed be all of that for many people, it doesn't have to be. I know, because over the past 30 years that I have been actively investing for my own retirement, I have developed an alternative way to think about investing. This approach (1) emphasizes things that we as investors have more personal control over, and (2) does not require such a "heroic" achievement in terms of earnings or stock performance as do typical growth-oriented strategies.

I call my strategy the Income Factory to focus attention on the actual job I expect my investment portfolio to do. That job is to produce a constant "river of cash"—that is, income—in the form of dividends and cash distributions that can then be reinvested in new securities, whose job in turn is to provide additional income in the future. As that new income is reinvested and begins producing even more income, my river of cash continually grows.

We discuss the math in more detail later, demonstrating how the cash buildup increases year after year at a fairly predictable rate, depending on the percentage yield our securities are paying us. The cash output from our Income Factory will double, then redouble, and then redouble again continuously over the course of one's lifetime. A 10% yielding portfolio doubles and redoubles about every 7.2 years. An 8% yielding portfolio doubles every 9 years, a 7% yielding portfolio almost every 10 years, and so on.

Notice I haven't said anything about the securities' market prices going up (or down). That's because an Income Factory's output (i.e., the cash it produces, which is constantly reinvested to produce more cash) does not depend much on the growth rate of its individual securities or even on whether they grow at all.

Instead, it is the reinvestment and compounding that provides the growth in the income stream, not any required growth in the dividends or market value of the assets in the portfolio. The portfolio, of course, grows in value over time, not because the individual securities rise in price, but because there are more of them as we use the cash we receive monthly or quarterly to buy more income-producing assets to add to our factory.

For those of us who grew up in an investing environment where market appreciation was the be-all and end-all, embracing the Income Factory's "growth without growth stocks" philosophy can be a big step, mentally and even emotionally. To make the leap of faith required, it is helpful to spell out and understand how growth actually occurs in a traditional investment portfolio.

First, note that the goal of most long-term investors (including me), regardless of what investment strategy we follow, is to earn an *equity return* averaging about 8% to 10% per year. We pick that target because 8% to 10% is approximately what returns on stocks have averaged over the past century. Some equity investors do better than that and others do worse, but if someone can match that average or even come close to it over a lifetime of investing, they (and their dependents and eventually their heirs) should be pretty happy later on when they reach and surpass retirement age.

The big question is how to achieve that 8% to 10% return. Return, or *total return* as it is often called, has two components: cash received (dividends or distributions paid by your securities) plus market price appreciation or depreciation. Cash received is real. Market price appreciation (or depreciation) is theoretical (paper profit or loss) and only becomes real when you sell the security and harvest the gain (or loss).

In traditional investing, you buy stocks that typically pay dividends of anywhere from 1% (sometimes zero) to 4% or 5%, and then depend on the company to make up the difference between that and your 8% or 10% target by increasing its earnings and dividends from year to year by the amount of the gap. The lower the cash dividend a company pays, the more its stockholders depend on future growth to reach their target earnings level. That's why a company that pays a paltry 1% or 2% dividend had better have serious growth prospects to make up the difference. A mature company, like a major utility or industrial "blue chip" that pays a more generous 4% to 5% dividend, has less of a gap between its dividend rate and its stockholders' 8% to 10% income target, but it is still expected to make up that 4% to 5% difference in growth year after year.

With our Income Factory strategy, we don't have a growth gap to worry about, since reinvesting and compounding the high cash distributions we receive achieves our total return target rate without requiring any additional market price growth. Our overall factory will in fact be worth more over time, not because prices of the individual securities grow, but because we can constantly use our cash income to purchase more of them, thus expanding the factory.

To better understand this, think of a real factory. When Ford Motor builds a new automobile plant, the only ones who care about what the plant is actually "worth"—that is, what Ford could sell it for—from day to day or month to month are the accountants. Everyone else at

Ford focuses on how many cars and trucks the plant produces, and how to increase that output going forward by reinvesting, adding new machines, and so on.

The market value of its plant is not relevant to Ford, since its business isn't buying and selling factories, it's making and selling cars. When we embrace an Income Factory strategy, we are acknowledging that our long-term investing goal is to create an income stream for ourselves. Owning stocks, bonds, funds, or other investments is a means to that end, which is creating the continually growing river of cash that we can retire on or use for other long-term goals. The Income Factory that produces that river of cash obviously has a very real *economic* value to us. But the price the market attaches to the Income Factory from day to day or even month to month is largely irrelevant to us as long-term investors.*

Later chapters get into more details about Income Factory strategies and how to set goals, implement a strategy, and monitor its success. We also discuss certain asset classes that are particularly suitable for this type of investing.

Three features of our strategy are especially attractive and should be mentioned here, even though we discuss them at length later on. One is the recognition that an Income Factory's earnings stream actually increases faster when stock markets are flat or dropping than when they are rising. This is intuitively difficult for many people to accept, since it flies in the face of our natural tendency to always assume that rising stock prices are a positive and make us wealthier.

The reality is that, for an income investor, your income stream doesn't drop just because stock prices do, so your river of cash buys more when securities have dropped and are "on sale" than when they rise. By being able to buy even more new securities (machines for the factory) because their prices have dropped than you would have been able to if prices

---

* The Income Factory strategy is appropriate for long-term investors looking to double, redouble, and continue to grow their investment portfolio and its income stream over a long period of time. If you are investing for the short term with the intention of liquidating your portfolio for a specific purpose like buying a house or paying for college within a few years, then this strategy is not for you, and you should focus on preserving your capital, even at the cost of failing to maximize your income stream.

were flat or had risen, you boost your compounding rate higher than it otherwise would be. The extra 0.5% or 1% you pick up by reinvesting through down markets over many years can eventually add tens of thousands of dollars of additional income. When Einstein said (reportedly although never confirmed) that "compound interest is the eighth wonder of the world," this is what he would have been talking about.

The second feature I like about our Income Factory strategy is the greater sense of security it gives us during periods of market turbulence. It is hard for many investors to sit through market slumps or bear markets and only collect the 2%, 3%, or 4% current yields that typical "growth" portfolios pay, while watching market prices fall. An Income Factory strategy, by employing investments and asset classes that pack a full equity return level of 8% to 10% into their cash distribution, makes it psychologically easier for investors to "keep the faith" and *not* feel the urge to get trigger happy and bail out or take defensive actions that might seem like a good idea—at first—but are costly over the long term.

In Charles Ellis's classic book on investing, *Winning the Loser's Game*, the author compares investing for many people to amateur—not professional—tennis, where he says most points are *lost* through bad shots as opposed to being *won* as a result of good shots. Ellis shows how this is also true in golf and even in war, where avoiding doing the *wrong* thing is the key to success much more than actually doing the *right* thing. In investing, doing the "wrong thing" typically involves losing one's nerve and selling out at what turns out to be a low point or even the bottom of a market slump. Such mistakes are often compounded by then "being on the platform and missing the train" when market prices turn up again, as history has shown us they eventually do.

The difference of seeing, feeling, and touching the cash each month that you can reinvest to create your own income growth, and especially to be able to do it all through the downturn itself, provides a sense of control that helps Income Factory investors fight off the impulse to "do something" that can involve turning temporary paper losses into permanent real ones.

Numerous studies demonstrate that buying quality stocks and holding them through thick and thin over many decades is the most effective way to achieve stock market success. But history shows many investors do *not* have the will forces and intestinal fortitude to buy and hold through market downturns. In this way, the Income Factory suits the psychological and emotional needs of many investors, as well as meeting their long-term financial objectives.

My other favorite feature of the Income Factory is that it allows, even encourages, what I call nonheroic investing. Think about the traditional "dividend growth" stock that pays cash dividends of 3% to 4% (or less) and has to then grow at 5% or 6% each year to make up the difference for an overall 8% to 10% growth rate. Since our entire economy is lucky to grow at about 3% per year, we know most companies can't be growing at almost twice that rate, unless they are like the children of *Prairie Home Companion*'s mythical Lake Wobegon, who were all reported to be "above average."

That means a typical growth investor expects all the stocks in his or her portfolio to have above average growth compared to the rest of the economy. Otherwise, why would their stock prices grow any faster than the economy at large? That to me is heroic investing, where you are expecting the securities you buy to substantially outperform their competitors and the economy in general. For that to happen, they have to be great companies and you have to be a great stock picker.

Securities in our Income Factory don't have to outperform. All they have to do is keep making the interest and dividend payments they already make. I consider that nonheroic investing. If it were a horse race, the heroic investments that expect above-average growth over time are the equivalent of betting on horses to win the race, or at least place or show, meaning they have to do much better than the average horse in the field. Our Income Factory horses only have to finish the race, that is, stay in business and make the interest and dividend payments they currently do. Which is the safer bet: betting on specific horses to win, place, or show, or betting on the entire field of horses to just finish the race?

By now you may be asking: "Sounds good, but if it is so obvious and straightforward, how come nobody else thought about it?"

Fair question. I think the answer is that it is easier to think outside the box about something if you have never been put inside the box to begin with. I never had any formal training in investing and never learned about traditional investment strategies until later in life. By then I'd already been an international banker and learned about credit and risk from the perspective of a lender, not a stockholder, so I was totally comfortable with the idea of making money via fixed-income payments (i.e., that stayed the same and never grew) rather than through stock price appreciation. For me it is all about math and probability. Which stream of payments will grow faster or more reliably? One that depends on heroic efforts on the part of companies to increase their cash flow over time, or one that relies on relatively nonheroic efforts by companies to merely maintain current cash flow levels?

Later I did a stint as a journalist at a financial magazine and learned how to write about complicated financial topics in plain English that nonexperts could understand. Hence my interest in using simple analogies like Income Factory or "betting on horses to merely finish the race instead of having to win, place, or show" to explain the difference between growth investing and an investment strategy based on cash-flow compounding. After that, I spent my third career in the financial markets working on products to assess the risk in corporate loans, private placements, and other nonpublic securities, which opened my eyes further to the risks and opportunities outside the traditional equity mainstream.

Finally, my experience during the "great crash" of 2007–2008 demonstrated, in my own portfolio and in the financial markets generally, how so many healthy assets that kept on pumping out cash flow just like the Energizer Bunny still dropped in market value to 50 or 60 cents on the dollar. This seared into my consciousness the idea that market price and paper profit (or loss) often have little to do with the real *economic* value of an asset, and that ignoring market prices while you keep your head down and continue to clip your coupons and reinvest through the storm can be critical to long-term success.

But you have to be invested in the right assets, for the right reasons, and with the right strategy. *The Income Factory* is all about how to do that.

How to Use
This Book

Readers may wish to think of this as essentially three books in one. In the first "book," which runs through Chapter 5, we describe the overall philosophy and strategy of the Income Factory, including (1) the basic idea that producing income is the primary purpose for most people's investing activities, (2) that reinvesting and compounding high cash distribution yields to produce income growth is every bit as effective as pursuing market price growth, and (3) that there are other less stressful and more predictable ways to generate an equity return than actually holding equity. After describing the Income Factory theory, the first book concludes, in Chapter 5, with a detailed look at the issues investors might consider in deciding whether an Income Factory strategy is appropriate for them, given their financial goals, investment style, risk/reward comfort level, and tax status.

Many investors may decide at this point that they don't need to read "book 2" (Chapters 6 through 9), which provides lists of possible candidate funds for assembling an Income Factory, including model portfolios of different sizes and risk/reward profiles. Once they grasp the philosophy and strategy, they may well conclude that they have all the information they need to go out and implement the strategy on their own. Other readers not yet prepared to do that may find the candidate fund list, model portfolios, and other earnings enhancement ideas in Chapters 6 through 9 to be helpful starting points.

The third book (Chapters 10 through 14) provides an in-depth discussion of the risks and rewards within the equity and fixed-income sectors, for readers who wish to have a more thorough understanding of the "bets" we are making when we invest in various asset classes, especially the ultra-high-yielding ones we may choose to hold modest positions in to boost our rate of return.

Finally in this chapter, there is a section on Income Factory maintenance with links to updated model portfolios and fund candidate lists on the Seeking Alpha blog site, which readers can access by pasting this address into their browser (https://seekingalpha.com/author/steven -bavaria/instablogs) or, if they prefer, searching online for "Steven Bavaria" or "Income Factory" to find links to related articles and blog posts.

* * *

The Income Factory has been written for an audience whose members may have a wide range of knowledge about, and attitudes toward, its subject. Readers may be at different places with respect to learning about, considering, accepting or rejecting, planning to implement, or actively employing an Income Factory strategy. The purpose of the book is to provide each reader with the insights, information, or tools they need, regardless of where they are on that spectrum.

There are three main themes underlying our Income Factory strategy:

1. Producing an *income* stream is the primary purpose of investing for most people and the public's fixation on the market value of the assets producing that income stream is a more recent phenomenon. The switch from focusing on income (which is more steady and predictable) to today's constant emphasis on market value has helped foster an enormous financial media and

investment management industry, but at the cost of increased stress and angst for average investors.

2. We can grow our income stream (and earn whatever target total return we set for ourselves) just as effectively through cash distributions as through market appreciation. In other words, "math is math," and we can earn a 10% equity return just as easily from a portfolio yielding 10% with 0% growth, as from one yielding 0% with 10% growth.

3. Combining those two concepts, we can easily conclude that we don't really need to hold equity to earn an equity return, if we can find other assets capable of providing that 10% yield we can use to reinvest and compound our income stream.

Surprising as it may seem, the ideas and conclusion embodied in these principles—that you can use high-yielding, nongrowth assets to build income and wealth over the long term—incurred stiff resistance from many writers and readers when I first introduced it on the Seeking Alpha website about five years ago. Despite the math being obvious and irrefutable, there was an emotional reaction from many who were convinced that growth was inconceivable and not authentic without growth stocks. Much of that initial resistance has been overcome, at least on the Seeking Alpha site, where over 9,000 followers and other readers continue to express their support for or at least their open-mindedness toward these principles that underpin the Income Factory strategy.

Chapters 2 through 4, plus the Introduction that you have already read, cover these themes and provide a top-down overview of the entire Income Factory strategy and the reasoning behind it. Chapter 2 lays out the intellectual foundation, presenting an overall rationale for how and why we invest, as well as an alternative way of measuring our own investment success that differs from the model that has been adopted, out of necessity rather than because it is logical, by the professional investing industry.

Chapter 3 goes on to describe how Mr. (or Ms.) Market translates economic performance into stock price movements. It explains how traditional investment strategies rely on the market to recognize corporate earnings and dividend growth and to convert that into equity prices, with considerable uncertainty about timing and a great deal of "wishing, waiting, and hoping" for it to happen. Then we introduce the Income Factory's approach of focusing on cash income rather than fixating on market price movement as an alternative many investors will find less stressful and easier to adhere to over the long term.

In Chapter 4 our focus shifts from describing the theory to being more of a how-to manual for readers who wish to further understand Income Factory principles as a prelude to incorporating it into their own investment strategy. We get a bit down and dirty (very briefly) in explaining the math underpinning the "reinvest and compound" approach to investing, even providing a link to a spreadsheet so readers can run their own yield-growth combinations and demonstrate it for themselves. Then we describe the various risk factors involved in both traditional growth investing and the Income Factory, and even introduce the option of an investor keeping a foot in each camp by blending the two approaches into an Income Factory Light (IFL) strategy that achieves some of the benefits of both. In Chapter 5 we turn to the practical aspects of designing an Income Factory that fits a reader's personal needs. That means considering financial goals, investment style, risk tolerance and comfort level, and the investor's tax situation, among other factors.

At this point, many readers may say, "Thanks, I get the idea. I'll take it from here." In other words, once they understand the theory and strategy, many investors will be perfectly capable of doing their own research and selecting the "machines" for their Income Factory on their own. But for those readers and investors who would like further practical ideas and direction, Chapters 6 through 9 contain lists of candidate funds for consideration, as well as model portfolios tailored to various risk/reward preferences, investment styles, and tax situations. I wish to caution readers that these lists of funds and other securities, indeed all the ideas expressed throughout the book, represent my good faith *opinions* at this point in time. I believe the Income Factory is an effective strategy, or I would not have committed most of my own savings to it or be relying on it to fund my own family's future. Nor would I have been doing it so publicly as I have been on Seeking Alpha, publishing the results like clockwork every quarter for many years. ("Eating my own cooking in public," I call it.)

Nevertheless, we must all realize there is no guarantee that any of the ideas, opinions, strategies, or specific funds or securities outlined here will lead to successful results in the future, either for myself or you. They represent insights I have accumulated over 50 years in finance and investing. And while many of the ideas have served me well in my own investing over many years, there is no assurance they will do so in a highly uncertain future.

With that understood, let us move on to specifics. In Chapter 6 we introduce a candidate list of 68 funds from 11 different asset classes, running the gamut from senior loans, high-yield bonds, and other fixed-income securities to more equity-oriented funds of various kinds, including real estate, utilities, master limited partnerships (MLPs), and equity-option funds, all of which have in common their propensity to pay higher yields than ordinary equity investments. From that candidate list, in Chapter 7 we present a number of model portfolios, some moderate in terms of their risk/reward characteristics and others more aggressive, that investors may wish to use "as is" or as a foundation for creating their own unique portfolios. The model portfolios allow investors to start with as few as 10 or 12 funds with moderate risk/reward profiles and the expectation of current annual distribution yields of about 8%, and to graduate up to larger and more aggressive portfolios with yields in the 10% range. Although the funds on the candidates' list and in the models are believed to be solid funds from respected fund families, we urge readers to do their own due diligence and check various investment sites for up-to-date pricing and yield data, as well as the most recent news and opinion articles on each fund. (I will be publishing routine updates of the model portfolios, available on the Seeking Alpha link cited elsewhere in this chapter.)

Chapter 8 begins with the observation that some investors "may decide to stop reading right here, and just get on with their investing," using the model portfolios as a starting point. But for those who wish to shoot for greater returns, the chapter describes ways to "soup up" their Income Factory with higher-yielding funds that also present a higher risk/reward profile. It describes the potential impact even a small increase in yield can have on our income growth over many years, while also explaining the trade-off in terms of additional downside risk. Chapter 9 presents other variations on the basic Income Factory theme, introducing a model portfolio for those who wish to pursue the IFL strategy mentioned earlier, as well as one for taxable accounts.

The next four chapters involve a deeper dive into the credit and fixed-income markets. They should be of interest to investors who really take seriously our idea of earning an equity return without investing in equity and want to understand in detail what that means and how we expect to do it. In these chapters, 10 through 13, we examine various asset classes, both fixed income and equities, to see what bets investors are actually making when they invest in them and how they are compensated for making those bets.

We begin by looking closely at the interest rate, credit, and equity bets that are embedded in stocks, bonds, and loans. We note how stockholders, whether they realize it or not, actually take all the risks of the loan and bond investors above them, as well as the additional existential risks of owning equity and being at the very bottom of the food chain if the company ever stumbles. This can come as a great surprise to equity investors who are happy to buy mid-cap and small-cap stocks (issued primarily by non-investment grade or even unrated companies), but say they wouldn't be caught dead buying so-called junk bonds, which are issued by the same cohort of companies (and are, in fact, less risky than the stock, which is worthless if the debt above it defaults).

In Chapter 12 we examine senior, secured corporate loans, a solid building block of an asset that plays a key role in our Income Factory portfolio. Loans are an attractive investment in their own right, and in Chapter 6 we include loan funds as one of the 11 asset classes in the candidate list of funds used to build our model portfolios. But loans are also pooled into more complex special-purpose vehicles called collateralized loan obligations (CLOs). Although CLOs are the principal buyers of all syndicated corporate loans, until recently they were limited to the portfolios of large institutional investors. CLO equity is still in its relative infancy as a retail investment, but a handful of funds specializing in CLO equity have appeared on the market within the past decade. They offer an opportunity to Income Factory investors willing to undertake the due diligence required to understand them, as well as take the additional risks that come with investing in ultra-high-yielding asset classes.

The CLO equity funds first mentioned in Chapter 8 are among our ultra-high-yielding vehicles of choice for enhancing (i.e., souping up) our risk/reward profile beyond the standard 10% equity return target of our aggressive portfolio models. Our goal in adding ultra-high yielders is to find that risk/reward sweet spot where we can boost our overall reinvestment and compounding rate by enough (0.5%, 1.0%, or more) to materially increase our ultimate income stream a decade or more in the future, but not so much as to cause serious downside damage if the ultra-high yields fail to sustain themselves and turn into more modest yields. That means keeping our total of ultra-high-yielding assets modest and, to the extent possible, well diversified.

Chapter 13 is for those readers who are intrigued enough by CLOs that they want a more comprehensive, yet still reasonably straightforward, description of them, how they work, and what issues to be aware of in investing in them. Readers who find all four of these chapters to be interesting—especially the more esoteric aspects of credit risk; the interplay between default, recovery, and ultimate loss; and how all of it affects ratings and pricing—may enjoy the story in the Appendix of the financial innovation that allowed loan assets to become accurately rated, priced, and—ultimately—securitized into CLOs.

For those who are still reading by Chapter 14, we return to the broader philosophical discussion of the first few chapters to connect the dots and describe how the Income Factory strategy fits logically into the classical investing canon extending back to Benjamin Graham in the 1930s. Once we accept the fact that (1) fundamentals definitely matter and are indeed incorporated into stock prices, (2) Mr. Market does this so efficiently that any analysis we do will already be built into the stock price by the time we can act on it, and (3) therefore, the best almost any of us can expect to achieve over the long term is to match the stock market average return, then we have to ask ourselves: why should we own stocks at all if we can achieve the same long-term result by investing in more predictable and less volatile asset classes that spare us the stress and overall angst of owning real equities?

Maintaining Your Income Factory

Factories require maintenance, and an Income Factory is no exception. While the economic and investment principles included here hopefully are relevant for many years to come, the model portfolios, especially the prices, distribution rates, and discounts or premiums on the funds included in them, change continually and need to be reviewed and updated. Our goal in selecting fund candidates for our model portfolios has been to make choices that are as timeless as possible, and we believe we have included solid performers managed by respected fund companies that could be parked in a well-diversified portfolio without requiring intensive monitoring.

Some investors may choose to put their Income Factory on autopilot and instruct their brokerage firms to reinvest all distributions back into the same funds that paid them. Given the diversification and the quality of the funds and fund managers, we expect such a strategy would accumulate a steadily growing income stream over many years, with routine monitoring and review. The downside risks would likely be occasional distribution cuts by one or another of the funds that would reduce the rate of cash distribution, reinvestment, and compounding.

More active investors want to monitor their portfolios (whether based on these models or otherwise) more frequently to keep an eye on distribution increases and decreases, unusual price movements, or changes in premium or discount levels that might suggest opportunities to rotate into similar funds that represent better values. To help them do that, I provide regular updates of the model portfolios that readers can access on my Seeking Alpha blog site: https://seekingalpha.com/author/steven-bavaria/instablogs or by searching online for "Steven Bavaria" or "Income Factory." Some are labeled "model portfolio updates" and others are reviews of the original Income Factory that I have been managing and reporting on for many years. Between the model portfolio updates and the other articles, there should be plenty of ideas for readers who want to tweak or otherwise update their Income Factories. Again, I urge readers to use my ideas as a starting point, but to do their own review and due diligence before pulling the trigger on purchases and sales within their own portfolios.

Why Do We Invest? What Makes Us Wealthy?

Throughout history, investments have been described in terms of the income they produce. It is an investment's income-generating capacity that drives both its economic value and, ultimately, its market price, not the other way around. But a huge, competitive money-management industry requires simple yardsticks for firms to use in showcasing and comparing their investment performance. Thus market price appreciation and "growth" have become paramount, even though they are less important to individual investors for whom the size of their income stream is more meaningful than whatever price Mr. Market assigns to the source of that income. Fortunately, retail investors do not have to fall for the drumbeat message from the financial media and professional investment community that market price appreciation is the quintessential goal. We developed the Income Factory as an alternative that allows investors to focus on building and capturing the *economic value* of their portfolios, irrespective of whatever price Mr. Market chooses to assign to them from one day to the next.

* * *

During most of our working lives, we focus on our income. How much money does a job pay us, or if we are considering a move, how much money will the *new job* pay us? It seems pretty straightforward.

It was certainly straightforward back in eighteenth- and nineteenth-century England, if you read the literature of the day. Life was brutal and not having the resources to survive was a constant theme from Charles Dickens to Jane Austen. The average person, as Bob Cratchit and his family knew so well, was just one pink slip away from the poorhouse. Even upper-class families of the sort Jane Austen described in novels like *Pride and Prejudice* and *Sense and Sensibility* were consumed with apprehension about their sons' and daughters' marriage prospects, driven by concerns about the income or lack thereof of their children and their children's prospective partners or suitors.

One thing I always found interesting in so many of these classic novels was how the wealth of various characters was usually defined in terms of their annual income. Mr. Darcy, for example, of *Pride and Prejudice*, is described as having "an income of £10,000 a year." The financial position of most characters, whether they have a lot of money or a little, is depicted in terms of the income their assets or estates produce, not by what those assets would reputedly be worth in market value terms. If Jane Austen's world had an annual *Forbes* Magazine's list of the world's richest people, it would have ranked them by their yearly incomes, not by the market value of their assets.

That makes total sense and certainly reflects how we think about ourselves and our own financial prospects. "How well we're doing" or how well our sons, daughters, relatives, and friends are navigating financially through life is almost invariably expressed in terms of our personal income. How much money are we or they making?

If we turn our attention to retirement planning, again the time-honored way to think about it has been in terms of income. Back in the day when companies provided traditional pensions because they expected their employees to work for them for most or all of their careers, *defined benefit* pensions promised employees a specific income stream. You worked so many years at an average salary of X, and you were then guaranteed a pension of a fixed amount when you hit a certain age. It was expressed as an annual income for a reason, since that was what employees could relate to and were used to thinking about in evaluating their own financial requirements. They could compare the anticipated pension payment directly with their current on-the-job salary and know how close their post-retirement income would come to replacing their preretirement income.

That's why so many of the personal financial products developed over the years have been of the annuity variety, where some financial firm would promise, for a fee (often an exorbitant one, although not always disclosed too clearly to the buyer), to pay clients a fixed amount of income for the rest of their lives. The financial firms developing and selling these products recognized that most consumers just wanted a predictable stream of income; they did not want to concern themselves with having to calculate the size of an investment portfolio capable of generating that income stream or having to assemble or manage the portfolio on an ongoing basis.

Income, Wealth, and Market Value

In the Donald Duck comic books I read as a kid, Donald had a rich uncle named Scrooge McDuck with a swimming pool literally filled with gold coins, and he would regularly go swimming in his pool of money. While wallowing in one's wealth, whether a pool of gold coins or a sizable portfolio at one's brokerage firm, is satisfying for some, for most of us the ultimate purpose of our wealth, especially our investments, is to generate an income stream that allows us to pay our bills and meet our other financial contingencies without worry or anxiety. In other words, it is the financial security and flexibility the income provides to us, not the market value, per se, of the invested assets, that makes us feel financially secure or even wealthy.

The rise of 401(k) plans, individual retirement accounts (IRAs), and other *defined contribution* retirement plans has dramatically changed the role of millions of investors, whether retired or planning to be at some point, as well as the way in which we all think about our invested assets. Previously we had professional investment firms responsible for managing the assets in our corporate pension plans, making sure they grew at a pace that would support the pension payments retiring employees had been promised.

Under defined contribution plans, the individual owners of the IRAs and 401(k)s have become their own pension plan managers, with no money management firms doing it for them as previously. Now the pension plan beneficiaries themselves (i.e., all of us) are responsible for making sure our own IRAs and 401(k)s are up to the task of providing us with the pension payments we will need in retirement. To paraphrase Walt Kelly's classic comic strip character Pogo, "We have met our pension plan and it is us."*

Having no big institutional third party promising—come hell or high water—that they will pay us retirement income of X dollars per month for the rest of our lives has profoundly changed the investment game for millions of people. One immediate result has been an explosion in retail investors' interest in the how-to of money management. And where have retail investors turned to learn how to invest their money more professionally? To the institutional investment professionals and a business and financial media schooled in traditional investment management dogma, all of them eager to share it with a vast new retail audience.

The biggest lesson retail investors are taught right away is that market value is the most important measurement of investment performance. Obviously, the media and market gurus pay enormous attention to it and expect their viewers to do so as well. Prices of various indices (Dow Jones Industrials, S&P 500, NASDAQ, Russell 2000, etc.) are displayed prominently and continually on every business news channel, and the latest price changes are reported as news

---

* Cultural historians and others may appreciate that cartoonist Walt Kelly created the phrase "we have met the enemy and he is us" and used variations of it in his Pogo comic strip from the 1950s through the 1970s. The phrase itself is a pun based on Commodore Oliver Perry's report to General (later President) William Henry Harrison of his victory over the British in 1813 in the Battle of Lake Erie that he had "met the enemy and they are ours."

updates throughout the day. With all this attention, it is no wonder individual investors have come to believe that market price is the main thing they should be focused on in managing their own investments.

Clearly the professional and institutional investment industry lives and dies by market value, with performance measured largely by how much the market prices of one's portfolio assets increase during a particular time period (monthly, quarterly, annually, etc.). "Total return," the most common performance measurement used, is the sum of market appreciation (or depreciation) and cash dividends received. But for most professionally managed stock portfolios (not our Income Factory), dividends are a relatively minor portion of the overall total return, with market appreciation (or depreciation) the major component.

Why does the investment community use market price appreciation as its primary performance measurement? The short answer is: What choice do they have? The investment management industry needs a common, easily understood benchmark. Market appreciation is simple, straightforward, easily calculated, and readily available.

Investment management is a highly competitive industry, and professional money managers constantly have to prove themselves and justify their value to clients, their investment committees, their boards of directors, or to whomever it is that makes decisions about how to compensate them or whether to continue with them or change to a new manager. In a similar way, mutual funds and other public investment vehicles have to compete constantly with other funds, asset classes, and investment products for the retail investor's business. So total return—which for most funds and firms is largely market appreciation—has become the standard industry-wide performance benchmark.

Just because market price performance is the simplest, most readily calculated, and easily understood answer to the performance question doesn't mean it is the correct or most relevant answer. The increase in value, reflecting the latest market price movements for the past week, month, or quarter, may reflect nothing whatsoever about the under-lying value of the companies whose stock is held, or their earnings or dividend-paying capacity. It may be merely "paper profit" that reflects random market sentiment influenced by political events, cyclical or seasonal factors, the weather, or other issues having little or no impact on the economic value of the holdings.

As retail investors managing our own money for our own purpose—to create and grow a cash income stream over a long-term horizon—we don't have to accept market appreciation and paper profit growth as the primary yardstick for judging our own performance just because the financial industry as a whole has chosen to do so for its own competitive purposes. In fact, the dirty little secret many professional investors would prefer us to ignore is this: market appreciation is *not* the most important factor in the growth of someone's personal portfolio.

To understand why not, we have to step back and review what it is that gives an investment—a stock, a bond, or whatever—its value. Where does value come from?

About 80 years ago an economist named John Burr Williams wrote a book called *The Theory of Investment Value* in which he articulated the idea that the "intrinsic value" of a security was the discounted present value of all the future cash flows that it would generate: primarily cash dividends and any residual value to be collected by selling the stock or winding up the business. Although less well known than Benjamin Graham and David Dodd, who had published their groundbreaking work (*Security Analysis*, 1934) on fundamental value investing a few years earlier, Williams's work complements theirs. Graham and Dodd emphasize using fundamental analytical methods to determine what a company's earnings and cash flows are likely to be, while Williams shows how—in theory—a rational market would value those earnings and cash flows. Together, their work explains and underpins the whole idea that stock markets are not casinos, as they were largely viewed in the 1920s, but are vehicles—albeit imperfect ones—for pricing and trading *investments* that have rational, determinable economic value.

The lesson for us in all this is that, ideally, the income should come first and then the market valuation will follow. In other words, the ability to generate an income stream is what drives the economic value of most assets (stocks, bonds, real estate, etc.), not the other way around. Once you know (or at least can make a good estimate about) the cash dividends that a security is likely to pay going forward, then you can calculate its theoretical intrinsic value (based on a number of factors, like how risky the security is, how fast its dividends are likely to grow, how high or low a discount rate should be applied to the future cash flows, etc.). But the point is, the income—both current and future—is the main thing that drives the security's value.

If I were a portfolio manager in a perfect world and could choose the yardstick I would like to be evaluated on, I would choose to be judged on how rapidly and consistently I grew my portfolio's income stream and *not* on how much its market value grew. If I consistently grew the income stream, then the value of the portfolio would be growing from an economic perspective (i.e., its usefulness to its owner, in the form of producing an income, would obviously be increasing), even if the market failed to recognize it and assign a higher price to it in the current quarter or reporting period. Using such a yardstick would better allow me to demonstrate my income-building skills as a portfolio manager, since analyzing and selecting securities for their income-generating capacity is something far more under my personal control than divining how much my securities are likely to go up or down in market price, which can happen for a myriad of reasons, few of them under my control or capable of being accurately forecast.

Of course, it would be very difficult to judge professional money managers across many different industries (pensions, endowments, mutual funds, hedge funds, etc.) on this sort of yardstick, even if the data could be collected and analyzed. So in an imperfect world that needs to find a common benchmark to judge professional money managers across the board, they have no choice but to chase the market appreciation target set by the industry in which they compete.

However, as personal investors, we have only one client we have to satisfy: ourselves. So we don't have to chase benchmarks that are not relevant to our long-term goals. If our long-term goal is to maximize the cash flow that our portfolio produces and to grow that river of cash as rapidly as possible from one year to the next, then we should formally set that as our specific objective, and not be goaded into pursuing a market appreciation strategy just because the larger investment world is hooked on it.

Does this mean our portfolio never grows in value because we are putting all our efforts into maximizing its cash income and not focusing on its current market price? No, but it means we aren't looking at every market movement—up or down—as somehow related to our securities' cash-generating abilities or deserving of some sort of action or reaction on our part. Instead, we recognize that the great majority of market changes—whether of the market as a whole or just the ups and downs of our specific holdings—are caused by random factors that have nothing whatsoever to do with our own securities' ability to continue making dividend or distribution payments. On big market movement days, when our friends and colleagues call us and say, "Hey, do you see what the market's doing? What are you going to do?" our response will probably be along the lines that we will continue to collect our dividends and look for opportunities to reinvest them at what are now bargain prices.

As we reinvest dividends to create ever-increasing income, the economic value of the investment portfolio generating those dividends grows as well, whether or not its market price immediately reflects that. If the market is rational, then our portfolio's market value should eventually rise to reflect its ever-increasing economic value. Whether it actually does or not is less important to us, however, since it is the income the portfolio generates that really matters, not how much the market values the portfolio generating it. In short, we don't have to worry about market prices but can put our efforts into reinvesting, compounding, and growing our income stream (and thus our economic value), while letting Benjamin Graham's Mr. Market catch up to us over the long run. Markets are not necessarily rational or predictable in the short term, but over the long term it is reasonable to expect that if our portfolio (our Income Factory) increases its *economic* value by continually producing more income for us, eventually its *market value* should reflect that as well. And it should if John Burr Williams, basic economic principles, and 80 years of history can be relied upon.

The Income Factory, both the theory and practice of which we describe in upcoming chapters, is the name I have given to the strategy of focusing on growing a portfolio's income stream and not worrying too much about how Mr. Market values the portfolio generating that income stream. In formulating this approach, I have drawn on several investment strategies institutional investors have used for decades, especially in the credit, high-yield, and alternative investment arenas, where they discovered long ago that achieving equity returns doesn't always require taking equity risks.

Besides borrowing from the credit, high-yield, and alternative investing universes, the Income Factory also builds on fundamental equity strategies that investors, both retail and institutional, have traditionally used to grow their incomes and portfolio values over time. These strategies—often labeled "value" or "dividend growth" or "total return" investing—typically depend on current dividend income for a portion of the total investment return, but expect most of that return to come from *future* growth of both the dividend itself and the stock price. I started out with a classic approach along these lines, and found it to be successful over a period of years in doing what it was supposed to do: grow my investment portfolio at an equity return (in my case over 10% on average for quite a number of years). But I did not enjoy the periodic "white knuckles" roller-coaster-ride aspects of it when the market was down; my portfolio was in neutral, reverse, or occasionally "free fall" mode; and I was gritting my teeth trying to decide whether to hold tight or take some sort of action.

That's when I began to migrate to what ultimately became the Income Factory strategy, writing about it as it evolved while also trying to "perfect" it. In many ways it remains a work in progress, although having thousands of readers on the Seeking Alpha investment site who have read my articles and embraced Income Factory principles in their own investment strategies suggests to me that we are on the right track.

In the next few chapters, we discuss the Income Factory more fully, as well as the more traditional strategy from which many of us "graduated" and which remains a viable, credible, and effective alternative for millions of investors. As we compare and contrast these approaches, we can see that no one investment strategy works for everyone; it is important to find the one that fits our own individual comfort level, as well as meets our personal financial goals.

How Mr. Market Captures Value

The Income Factory presents investors with a different way of thinking about their investment philosophy, strategy, and ultimate goals. Like traditional "value" or "dividend growth investing" strategies, it aims at building wealth over a long period of time, but as outlined in the last chapter, it chooses to define wealth in terms of the income it delivers rather than in value as measured by market price. Both strategies involve risks, and investors invariably believe the risks they are less familiar with are worse than those they are more accustomed to. One of the main reasons its advocates find the Income Factory attractive is its relative simplicity compared to the more complex way in which traditional dividend growth strategies "harvest" corporate growth in earnings and dividends and then eventually "convert" it into stock market value and total return. For that to happen, Mr. Market first must recognize that a company has increased its earnings and dividends, and then readjust the company's stock price to maintain its price/earnings ratio and yield parity with the stock of comparable companies, all within a macro framework in which extraneous political, economic, and financial concerns may be creating adverse or countervailing effects. With so many moving parts, it is no wonder many investors find it too stressful to "stay the course" and end up losing out on the demonstrated benefits of long-term equity investing. By focusing single-mindedly on the steady growth of cash income, the Income Factory presents a simpler model for both defining and harvesting a long-term equity return. Investors also find it psychologically and emotionally easier to sit tight during turbulent times if they see the cash rolling in steadily even as market prices fluctuate.

*   *   *

The Income Factory is an alternative to the traditional value or dividend growth investing strategies that millions of investors use in building wealth to meet their retirement or other long-term needs. As noted earlier, the main difference between the Income Factory and other traditional strategies is that:

- Traditional strategies invariably rely on individual stocks to grow both their dividends and their stock prices over time to create the growth in the overall portfolio.
- The Income Factory does not expect or require the individual securities it holds to grow their dividend payments or their stock prices. Instead, it uses the cash dividends it receives to create the portfolio growth, by constantly reinvesting and compounding them to buy new securities and "grow the factory."

Income Factory advocates do not claim it is better than traditional investing strategies or that it will generate higher returns. All we claim is that it is a legitimate alternative and is just as likely to generate *equity returns* over the long term as traditional strategies. Its primary advantage is psychological and emotional, as much as it is financial. Many investors are uncomfortable with the market volatility and uncertainty inherent in traditional growth-based strategies, especially the heart-dropping roller-coaster experience of holding stocks and other investments through bear markets or crashes like we had in 2008.

The Income Factory does not eliminate investment angst and uncertainty. But focusing on the cash income produced (which is relatively predictable), rather than on the market price level (which is not), is less stressful for investors, and the high level of cash generated on a regular basis cushions both the psychic and economic impact of market downturns. This in turn makes it less likely investors will lose their nerve and cash out during stressful periods, only to find themselves standing on the sidelines when Mr. Market decides to fire up his engines again. Unfortunately, in investing there is no conductor to call out "all aboard" before the train starts moving out of the station, and being left behind after jumping off the investment train out of fear of loss is one of the major "wealth killer" mistakes that retail investors make.

Alternative Strategies, Alternative Risks

The key to understanding the Income Factory strategy and how it relates to and differs from a more traditional investing strategy is to understand that "total return" has two elements: cash received as dividends or distributions, and market appreciation or depreciation. If a stock pays you a 5% cash dividend and its stock price also increases by 5%, then your total return is the sum of the two, or in this case, 10%. Although the two elements—dividend yield and price growth—are equally important and relevant, price growth has always been the more glamorous and closely followed of the two. CNBC, Bloomberg, and Fox Business News report all day long about price movements in major indices, like the Dow Jones Industrial Average, or the S&P 500, or the stock prices of major companies, with little attention to dividends paid or changed. That's not surprising, since price movements are highly visible, are transparent, and can be exciting when they are sudden, large, or both. Tracking dividends, compared to following price movements, is like watching paint dry.

But just as in baseball, where a run scored on a single counts just as much as one scored on a towering home run, total return achieved through cash dividends counts just as much as total return resulting from market price increases. However, the investment bet involved in an Income Factory investment is somewhat different than the investment bet being made by a traditional total return or dividend growth investor. Many investors do not fully understand the bets they are making when they buy different types of stocks, bonds, or other asset classes, or what has to happen for them to win—or lose—those bets. Or they may understand the bet they are making with one type of stock or asset class, and then assume that the bet is the same, or the risk is the same, when moving to some other asset class.

In this chapter we begin to examine the sets of assumptions and the risks that underpin both strategies. First, we take a detailed look at the investment bet being made by followers of a traditional dividend growth strategy. We describe how corporate *business* performance gets translated into *market price* performance, and how a lot of things—some of them "micro" and within the control of individual companies, and others "macro" and outside of their control—need to line up just right for that to happen. We also discuss how the uncertainty and frequent disconnect between a company's business reality and its stock price can be so disconcerting and stressful to many investors that it risks undermining their ability to develop and follow through with prudent long-term strategies.

An Income Factory strategy, as we explore in more detail in the next chapter, carries risks of its own. But the two strategies—traditional total return/dividend growth and Income Factory—are different enough that individual investors may well find one or the other to be more compatible with their personal level of risk tolerance. The aim is not to convince readers that one strategy is better than the other, but to help readers appreciate they have more than one path to choose from to get to the same long-term investing goal.

It is not surprising that the debate between Income Factory adherents and fans of traditional dividend growth investing often comes down to a "my risk is better than your risk" discussion. That probably reflects the fact that people are typically more comfortable with risks they are familiar with than with ones they are not. I suspect lion tamers generally think they have safer jobs than trapeze artists, and vice versa.

How Dividend Growth
Becomes Stock Price Growth

Let us begin with how traditional stock investors build wealth. Virtually all long-term equity investors—regardless of whether we employ an Income Factory or traditional strategy—seek to earn an "equity return" of about 8% to 10%, which is the average return to investors in common stocks over the past century or so. As noted earlier, the difference between the two approaches is that while Income Factory investors look to reinvesting and compounding current cash income as the main source of their long-term growth, traditional dividend growth investors expect to earn their 8% to 10% return through a combination of cash dividends and stock price appreciation that is heavily weighted toward price appreciation.

Typically the blue chips and other dividend growth stocks owned by traditional stock investors pay 2% or 3% in current dividend yield and the investor expects to receive the other 6% or 7% in the form of annual dividend growth, which would translate itself into stock price appreciation as the market eventually rewards the company for increasing its dividend by raising its market price. That's what is supposed to happen, and dividend growth investors have every right to expect it to happen if the market behaves rationally. Generally stock markets do act rationally, *over the long run*, but it doesn't always happen right away or automatically. Here is how it is supposed to work, at least in theory.

Suppose a company's stock has been paying a dividend of $1 per annum and selling at a price of $25, pretty consistently for some time. Its yield is 4%, since $1 divided by $25 equals 4%. That means Mr. Market, after weighing up all the information about the company—its business, its financial stability, its earnings, its growth—has concluded that from an overall risk/reward standpoint it matches up with other companies whose stock is priced to yield 4%, and has therefore priced it accordingly.

Now suppose the company raises its dividend by 5%, which in this case would be from $1 to $1.05. If its price remained at $25, the new dividend rate would be $1.05 divided by $25, or 4.2%. But the market has already determined, from a risk/reward standpoint, that to induce investors to buy and hold the stock, the company only needs to pay them a dividend of 4%. So what is likely to happen is that, in the hours, days, or weeks after the new dividend rate is announced, the share price moves up to $26.25, bringing the yield back down to 4% (since $1.05, the new dividend rate, divided by $26.25, the new market price, is 4%).

When the holders of the stock calculate their return for this period, they have earned a total return of 9%, part of it from the cash dividend yield, which is still 4%, and the rest from the market price appreciation of 5% (i.e., the increase from $25 to $26.25, a 5% rise in price). Also note that when the market reprices the stock to a level that maintains the same yield as before the dividend increase (which it should if nothing else about the company has changed), then the percentage increase in the market price (5%) matches the percentage increase in the yield (also 5%).

Notice the key assumption about the market being *rational*. If it is rational and "other things remain equal," which they don't always do, then a certain percentage change in a stock's dividend payout should translate into an equivalent percentage change in the stock's market price. That is a critical tenet of a traditional dividend growth strategy. Another way to think about it is that a rational market recognizes change in the underlying *economic* value of a stock (i.e., the amount of income it generates) and reflects it in the stock's *market* value, if not immediately, then in the long run.

As you can see, in the preceding example, if the company manages to increase its dividend 5% every year and the market translates that into a 5% appreciation in its stock price, when you combine that with the 4% annual cash yield from the dividend itself, you have a total of 9% in total return. If reinvested and repeated year after year, that would more than satisfy most long-term investors. To be specific, reinvesting and compounding a 9% return every year would double the size of the investment portfolio in 8 years, redouble it again in another 8 years, and so on.

Every investor should understand the Rule of 72, which is a quick and approximate way to determine how quickly a stream of income or the value of a portfolio doubles when reinvested at any particular rate of return. You divide the rate of return into 72, and the answer is the approximate number of years in which your income stream or portfolio value doubles, when reinvested and compounded. At 10% your portfolio or income stream doubles in just over seven years. At 7%, it doubles in about 10 years, and so on. If we project out over an investment horizon of many decades, we see that every extra 0.5% or 1% that an investor manages to add to their long-term total return makes a huge difference in terms of how much income or portfolio wealth they accumulate over a lifetime of investing.

Using the Rule of 72, here are the results if we reinvest and compound a total return at the following rates for 40 years, starting with $10,000:

- At 7%, $10,000 doubles about every 10 years, and grows to approximately $150,000 after 40 years, 15 times its original amount.
- At 8%, $10,000 doubles every 9 years, and grows to $220,000 after 40 years, 22 times its original amount.
- At 9%, $10,000 doubles every 8 years, and grows to $310,000 after 40 years, 31 times its original amount.
- At 10%, $10,000 doubles about every 7 years, and grows to $450,000 after 40 years, 45 times its original amount.

The Rule of 72 is a handy, albeit approximate, tool for estimating the impact of yields and reinvestment rates on our investment results over long periods of time. It shows, for example, that a 25-year-old who starts with a $10,000 portfolio, reinvests and compounds it, could have a $220,000 portfolio by age 65 if they managed to average an 8% return over a typical 40-year working life. If they were more aggressive and averaged a return of 9%, they could end up with over $300,000, and if they achieved a 10% return, they could reach $450,000, more than double what they accumulate at "only" 8%. (Of course, this tells only part of the story, since the average investor will be adding more money to their portfolio over the years. This, in turn, will create additional earnings to be reinvested and compounded.)

We say "only 8%" because 8% is actually a very respectable long-term rate of return and greater than what the average investor manages to achieve. But because the effects of reinvesting and compounding are so powerful in long-term wealth and income accumulation, it is worth seeking that extra percentage point or two, if we can find a way to do so that is reasonable and prudent from a risk/reward standpoint. As shown previously, a 2% difference in return over a lifetime of investing can mean actually *doubling* the amount of income or total savings that an investor has leading into retirement. That is why it is so important to not settle for that so-called safe annuity that pays only 6%, or, equally important, not to mindlessly follow some outdated investment formula (e.g., 60% stocks, 40% bonds) because some "advisor" recommends it. Playing it safe can mean retiring on half the income (or less) than one might otherwise have by playing it smart, which if done wisely can also be safe.

The Rule of 72 works whether you are compounding an annual rate of return that comes totally from market price growth alone (i.e., no cash dividends, but all the return from price appreciation), or totally from cash dividends (i.e., no growth in the stock price, the entire return from cash payments to shareholders), or from a blend of the two approaches. It doesn't matter where the total return comes from. If you reinvest and compound it, the Rule of 72 will tell you how fast it grows.

Expecting a Lot from Mr. Market

We described earlier how Mr. Market translates actual corporate performance, particularly increases in the dividend payment rate, into stock values. Of course, dividends are not the only corporate action that affects the stock price. The other major one is corporate earnings, with the price/earnings ratio, or P/E ratio, being the most critical yardstick, along with the dividend yield, for comparing and projecting stock prices. Since dividends are paid out of earnings, the two ratios generally move in tandem, at least over the long run, and dividend increases are often preceded by earnings increases.

As a dividend growth or value investor, you are always happy to see both earnings increase and dividends increase. Either one is likely to lead to stock price increases, as explained earlier. Just as Mr. Market will likely increase a stock's price when its dividend increases, to maintain its dividend yield at the previous level, so will it also tend to increase the stock price of a company whose earnings have increased, to maintain its price/earnings ratio at its previous level.

Of course, Mr. Market may sometimes change its mind about a particular company and begin requiring or tolerating a different blend of dividend increases and earning increases. For example, a company that began growing its earnings at a faster rate than it had done historically might find the market beginning to perceive it as more of a growth company, with investors willing to buy and hold it at a higher price in relation to both its earnings and its dividends than previously. That would mean Mr. Market is saying, "We see you are growing your earnings faster than you previously did, and if you are prepared to continue doing that, then investors will be content to pay a higher price (i.e., higher P/E ratio) and accept a lower current dividend yield, in anticipation of your faster earnings growth in the future." In other words, investors want the same long-term total return of 10% that they previously did, but now they are willing to accept less of it in current cash dividends because they are confident they will get more of it in future earnings and dividend growth.

Sometimes this process happens in reverse and a company previously considered a growth company slows down and matures, in which case the market may begin to require a higher dividend yield to offset the reality that the company isn't likely to be growing as fast in the future as it previously did. In this case, investors as a whole (whether they realize it or not) are saying, "We want our equity return and if we aren't going to be getting as much of it through earnings growth and future stock price appreciation, then we want more of it in current cash."

Companies themselves have some control over this dynamic. Management may decide to use a portion of its cashflow to buy back its own stock, rather than pay out the cash as a dividend. This essentially converts what would have been a direct cash distribution to stockholders into a potential capital gain. By buying back its stock, the company is decreasing the number of shares outstanding, which increases its earnings per share (EPS). Assuming Mr. Market decides to maintain the same price/earnings ratio on the stock, the stock price (the numerator in the P/E ratio) should adjust upward as the earnings per share (the denominator) increase as a result of the buyback. Buybacks, by increasing the stock price rather than paying out cash to shareholders, are particularly attractive to CEOs and other executives with stock options whose payout depends exclusively on stock appreciation rather than on total return.

What we described previously—the market's constant observation of the earnings and dividends of a company and its adjustment of the stock price to reflect it—is the traditional, often unstated or not even realized, assumption behind most people's investment in corporate stocks and their expectation the value will grow to reflect the underlying economic reality. And generally it works. An investor builds a portfolio of a diversified cross-section of companies in different industries and then harvests the increased value created as the companies, or at least most of them (that's why you diversify), grow their businesses, their earnings, and their dividends over the years. All of which is ultimately captured and reflected in their stock prices, as the market recognizes the growth in these key performance indicators and eventually rewards the companies for it by bidding up their shares.

It sounds straightforward and, as mentioned elsewhere, reality has actually matched the theory over the long run, with Mr. Market doing a pretty good job of recognizing and capturing real economic value and incorporating it in market prices. But it is a complex model where a lot has to happen. The investor has to pick the right stocks or asset class and be willing to sit and wait patiently for the companies to improve their performance. Then once the companies actually manage to increase their earnings and dividends, the market has to recognize it and increase their stock prices accordingly. In this way, the dividends and stock prices inch their way up, slowly and steadily over time.

To me, as an investor trained originally, first in law school and then later as a banker who handled "workouts" and bankruptcies, to focus on all the things that can go wrong, the traditional investment value proposition seems like it has a lot of moving parts, failure of any of which can "derail the train" and prevent the investment from being successful. Let's list them:

- The companies whose stocks you pick have to grow their earnings and dividends by the 6% or 8% per annum rate (about *twice the growth rate* of the economy as a whole) required to meet historical equity growth targets of 8% to 10% (when added to their dividend yield of 2% or 3%).
- Then they must repeat the performance year after year on a sustained basis.
- Then the market has to recognize that growth and increase each company's stock price to reflect the performance appropriately.
- Finally, we have to hope that there are no bear markets, macro events, or other extraneous occurrences—economic, financial, or political—that would cause the market to drop or stagnate, offsetting our company's positive performance and thwarting or delaying its stock's upward progress.

Those are the substantial hurdles a dividend growth investment strategy faces. What's really impressive is that the strategy works in spite of them. That is, it works over the long term. All the data and literature demonstrate clearly that, at least historically, if you bought a diversified portfolio of stocks—whether growth stocks or value stocks; mid-caps, small-caps, large-caps; indexed or actively managed—and held them for decades, in most cases you would have achieved the 8% to 10% average returns that equity ownership has historically provided.

But the key to success is holding for the long term. Moving in and out of the stock market, even during long periods where the market is in an upward trend, has been shown to hurt your chances of success versus staying fully invested all the time. For example, studies have shown that if you invested in stocks and stayed fully invested for random 20-year periods over the past 40 years, depending on which 20-year period you picked, your average annual return, even if you picked the *worst* possible 20-year period, would have been a moderately below average 6%. And if you picked the *best* possible period, it would have been 18%. In other words, being in the market and staying in the market works and is the secret to long-term wealth accumulation. Put another way, it is actually hard to screw up a long-term investment strategy, if you buy, hold, and ignore it for long enough periods. Rip Van Winkle would have been a successful money manager.

But the same studies show that if you got in and out of the market at random times over that 40-year period, never staying in for as long as 20 years, then your performance would have varied all over the lot, with greatly increased chances of both outsized gains and huge losses.

Most investors have heard this over and over again and know it is true. But they still get antsy and worried when the market tanks and they see their portfolio dropping in value day after day. That to me is the biggest risk with traditional dividend growth investing. Not that the strategy doesn't work over the long term *if you stick to it*, but that the short term can be so scary for so many investors that they bail out and never get to experience the long-term benefits. A good example of this was the great crash of 2008. Many investors (like the author) were smart and/or lucky enough to hold on tight, collect dividends, and reinvest at bargain prices all through the crash, eventually seeing large gains when markets recovered and heavily discounted assets returned to par a year or so later. But there were many others who got scared, moved to the sidelines at the worst possible time, and missed the opportunity of a lifetime.

The Income Factory refocuses our attention on the cash flow that keeps rolling in month after month regardless of what market prices are doing, thus making it easier—psychologically and emotionally—for investors to ignore market volatility that can otherwise be so stressful and distracting. But that doesn't mean it has no risks of its own. The

Income Factory's risks have more to do with finding the right assets, ones that can keep paying at a steady rate forever, than with worrying about growth, the markets, and what moves stock prices.

Fortunately, once you change your focus to income generation instead of market price growth, more asset classes and investment vehicles become available and you are no longer limited to "the usual suspects" in the equity investing world. In the next chapter we explore in more detail both the differences and similarities between Income Factory and traditional total return portfolios, including how some investors may manage to harness the advantages of both strategies at once. We may even find that some investors already have an Income Factory and don't realize it.

Income Factory

The Math, the Risks, and the Choices

The Income Factory's basic idea—that you can achieve long-term growth solely through high-yield cash distributions without any dividend or stock price growth—met a great deal of skepticism and denial when first introduced several years ago. But "math is math," and we can demonstrate conclusively that a total rate of return—whether a rate of 10% or any other rate—can be achieved by whatever combination of annual dividend yield and annual dividend growth adds up to the chosen rate. Even after demonstrating it, as we do in this chapter, old attitudes die hard and many investors will continue to want to see their portfolio growth be driven by a combination of cash dividend yields and individual stock price growth. That, of course, is fine because the purpose of the Income Factory is not to "win converts" but to present a viable alternative to the traditional total return or dividend growth strategy that has worked successfully over the long term but can lead to a lot of angst and nail-biting in the short term. As we explore the risks of both strategies—the Income Factory and traditional dividend-growth investing—we see there are aspects of both that may appeal to many investors. Some traditional investors may find, when they examine their current portfolios, that they already have elements of an Income Factory and don't even realize it. For them, an Income Factory Light (IFL) strategy may be sufficient to provide them with the confidence and staying power required to ride out market storms, while others may prefer to totally embrace the Income Factory approach. Later on, we provide model portfolios and asset class suggestions for whichever option readers select.

* * *

Growth Portfolio Versus Growth Stocks

The essence of an Income Factory strategy, and what differentiates it from traditional equity total-return strategies, is that it derives all (or virtually all) of its total return from the cash dividends and distributions it receives, and expects to receive virtually none of it from capital appreciation. That means it generates all of its growth from reinvesting and compounding its high-yielding cash distributions, with no internal or organic growth from within the individual stocks or securities themselves. All it asks from its individual securities is static but stable performance—that they continue indefinitely making the dividend or interest payments they are already making, with no growth expected or required.

We refer to the portfolio as an Income Factory to reinforce the point that its sole function is to produce its factory output, which is a river of cash that we reinvest and compound to produce future growth. We do not pay much attention to the market value of the factory (or of the individual machines in it), any more than anyone at Ford Motor (except the accountants) pays attention to the market value of its automobile plants. What Ford focuses on is the output of its factories—how many cars and trucks they produce, and how to grow that number through reinvesting and upgrading them. Similarly, we do not expect the "machines" in our factory (i.e., the individual securities) to increase their dividends or distributions. Instead we grow the factory itself (and its annual output) from one year to the next by reinvesting the cash output it produces in "new machines" (additional securities).

As we saw in the last chapter, a typical dividend growth or other total return-based strategy buys stocks that pay minimal dividends, perhaps 2% to 4%, and then expects to get the rest of its equity return of 8% to 10% from annual growth of the dividend by another 5% or 6%, which eventually gets recognized by the market and translated into a higher stock price. The Income Factory strategy would look for stocks and other investments that pay out 8% to 10% in dividends or distributions, thereby getting its entire targeted equity return in cash and not having to worry about whether it gets any of it from dividend growth and market appreciation. The two strategies are making two different investment bets and taking different risks:

- The typical dividend growth or total return investor is primarily betting on companies to *grow* their earnings and dividends, which in turn will cause their stock prices to grow and the value of their total portfolio to grow.
- Income Factory investors are not expecting the companies whose securities they buy to grow their earnings and dividends, but are betting on their *continuing* to make the same payments (dividends, distributions, or interest payments) they currently do; their portfolios and the ongoing cash distributions they generate will grow from reinvesting and compounding those payments.

The first investor is making a traditional equity bet that the companies whose stock they buy will excel, growing by enough each year to provide a steady 8% to 10% equity return. If the company manages to do that, the investor wins the bet. The Income Factory investors are making more of a credit bet than an equity bet, since they expect and require no performance growth, but are merely counting on the companies whose securities they buy to continue the current level of dividends, distributions, or interest payments they are already making.

There are obvious risks to each type of investment bet, which we discuss later on.

Math Is Math, But Old Habits Die Hard

Disregarding whatever difference in risks there may be between the two strategies, from a mathematical standpoint you can earn a total return of 10% just as readily from (1) a portfolio paying out a 5% dividend and earning the remaining 5% through growth of its stock price, as from (2) earning the entire 10% in cash via dividend payments. If you reinvest and compound both portfolios, they will each grow at the same rate and at the end of whatever period of time you choose, the two portfolios will have the same total market value.

Of course, you will have arrived at that point by different routes. The growth portfolio will end up with fewer shares, but each will be worth a lot more because its share price will have grown at a high rate over the years as its dividends and earnings per share grew. The Income Factory will have grown its number of shares by far more, through reinvesting and compounding, but each share won't be worth any more than it was at the start, since each will be paying the same cash dividend and there will be no reason for the share price to increase.

When you multiply the growth portfolio's fewer number of shares times the increased value per share, and compare it to the Income Factory's greater number of shares multiplied by their static value per share, you get the same current market value for each portfolio. And indeed you should, if each portfolio has been generating a total return of 10% per year, albeit by using different investing tactics.

That two portfolios employing such radically different tactics could achieve the identical total return and have the same market value at the end of 10 years (or any other period) has been difficult to accept by investors and commentators brought up on a steady diet of total return and growth, whether dividend growth, earnings growth, or market price growth. The popular wisdom, for many years, has been that earnings and dividend growth are absolutely necessary to achieve the sort of equity return required to create and accumulate long-term wealth. When I first began writing about this strategy and calling it the Income Factory, proponents of traditional total return and dividend growth strategies insisted it wasn't possible or feasible to invest in high-yield, no-growth assets and keep up with a portfolio of stocks that continually increased their dividends.

The largely unexamined assumption underlying these arguments was that a growth stock strategy of some sort was necessary and appropriate during the accumulation phase of investing (perhaps ages 20 to 50 or so), and that a strategy emphasizing yields and cash flow was only appropriate for older investors approaching or already in retirement. Younger investors, especially, were encouraged to seek out quality blue chips, whether current or potential, that had records of steady, continuing growth and were expected to maintain them into the future. There are a number of popular lists, with names like "Dividend Champions," "Dividend Kings," and "Dividend Aristocrats," all including companies with solid, consistent records of dividend payment and growth. They contain lots of familiar names, like Colgate Palmolive, Emerson Electric, Johnson & Johnson, Kimberly-Clark, Illinois Tool Works, McDonalds, Wal-Mart, Clorox, and many others. Most of them pay dividends in the 2% to 3% range, but grow them steadily. The expectation, of course, is that these companies will grow their dividends by 5%, 6%, 7%, or more each year, thus bringing the entire portfolio growth up to an equity return level of 8% to 10%. Finding such companies and investing in them has indeed been a successful long-term strategy over many years.

It is human nature to believe that something that has worked well for so many people in the past is, therefore, the best approach for everyone. But as we pointed out in the last chapter, there are risks even with a tried-and-true strategy like long-term dividend growth investing. The risk isn't that it won't work for those willing and able to commit to it for the long term. The real risk, in my experience, is that some investors will panic and bail out in tough, turbulent times and "miss the train" when it starts up again, thus losing out on the long-term equity market growth that history has shown is there for those investors patient enough to harvest it.

The Income Factory does not claim to be a better strategy than traditional total return investing, but rather is a legitimate alternative that may appeal to investors for whom the waiting and hoping for growth to occur that is required in traditional investing may be too stressful or difficult, especially when markets are declining. With the Income Factory strategy, the river of cash that our high-yielding Income Factory churns out through all sorts of markets can be a strong psychological and emotional buffer to the paper losses all portfolios suffer during periods of market anxiety.

I developed the following examples as a way to demonstrate that the math works, and that total return is total return, no matter how you achieve it. They show how portfolios would perform with various combinations of dividend yield and growth. There is a link to download the spreadsheet for those who wish to change the assumptions or input their own.

The bottom line result is that, whatever total return target you choose, you can achieve it by any combination of (1) dividend yield and (2) market price appreciation that adds up to that total return. Therefore, either method is just as appropriate for an investor—whether 25 or 65—who is seeking that target return. They are equally valid ways to earn, say, 10% per year if that is your long-term target. The key is to pick a strategy that makes sense for you—psychologically and emotionally as well as financially—and stick with it over time. Here are three illustrative examples.

Portfolio A (a growth-oriented portfolio) starts off with a single stock that sells for $100 and pays a dividend of $2 for a yield of 2%. Each year the stock increases its dividend by 8%, and the market increases the stock's price by 8%, which keeps the dividend yield steady at 2%. The total return to Portfolio A is therefore 10% (i.e., 2% from its dividend yield and 8% from the dividend growth and matching stock appreciation). So going into the second year, the annual dividend has increased 8% to $2.16, and "Mr. Market" has increased the stock price to $108, matching the 8% increase in the dividend and keeping the yield at 2%.

TABLE 4.1 Portfolio A: Low-Dividend/High-Growth Strategy

Years	# of Shares at Start of Period	Share Price at Start of Period	Div. Rate (yield)	Div. Growth Rate	Div. Rate ($$) per Share	Next Year's Div. Rate	New Stock Price in Response to New Dividend Rate	This Year's Div. Income	This Year's Stock Price Increase Due to Dividend Increase	This Year's Total Return in $$$	This Year's Total Return %	# of New Shares Bought with Reinvested Dividend
1	1.00	100.00	2.0%	8.0%	2.00	2.16	108.00	2.00	8.00	10.00	10%	0.02
2	1.02	108.00	2.0%	8.0%	2.16	2.33	116.64	2.20	8.80	11.00	10%	0.02
3	1.04	116.64	2.0%	8.0%	2.33	2.52	125.97	2.42	9.68	12.10	10%	0.02
4	1.06	125.97	2.0%	8.0%	2.52	2.72	136.05	2.66	10.65	13.31	10%	0.02
5	1.08	136.05	2.0%	8.0%	2.72	2.94	146.93	2.93	11.71	14.64	10%	0.02
6	1.10	146.93	2.0%	8.0%	2.94	3.17	158.69	3.22	12.88	16.11	10%	0.02
7	1.12	158.69	2.0%	8.0%	3.17	3.43	171.38	3.54	14.17	17.72	10%	0.02
8	1.14	171.38	2.0%	8.0%	3.43	3.70	185.09	3.90	15.59	19.49	10%	0.02
9	1.16	185.09	2.0%	8.0%	3.70	4.00	199.90	4.29	17.15	21.44	10%	0.02
10	1.18	199.90	2.0%	8.0%	4.00	4.32	215.89	4.72	18.86	23.58	10%	0.02
Totals								31.87	127.50	159.37		

49

Every year the dividend is reinvested in new shares at their new price, so the following year the total return of the portfolio (in dollar terms) increases as a result of the capital appreciation from the stock price increasing, and from the increased dividend income from the additional shares owned as a result of reinvesting that year's dividend. For Portfolio A, over time, the annual growth in portfolio value of 10% is driven mostly by the 8% annual capital appreciation (due to the dividend growth), and to a lesser extent by reinvesting the 2% dividend to buy new shares at the higher price. The cumulative total return, over 10 years, of $159.37, is comprised of 20% dividend income and 80% stock price appreciation, exactly in proportion to the 2% yield and 8% dividend growth of the portfolio.

As we consider other examples, we shall see that any combination of yield and growth that adds up to 10% provides us with the same total return, but with a different proportion of the return coming from dividend income and stock appreciation.

Portfolio B is a more balanced income/growth portfolio. It starts off again with a single stock selling for $100, but this time it pays a dividend of $5 for a yield of 5%. With a higher yield than Portfolio A's stock, we don't expect Portfolio B's dividends to grow as fast, and we assume a dividend growth rate of 5%. So Portfolio B's total return of 10% is derived from a 5% cash yield plus another 5% dividend growth, which we assume Mr. Market recognizes and incorporates into the stock's market price. Going into its second year, Portfolio B, like Portfolio A, owns additional shares (having reinvested its $5 dividend, which buys more shares than Portfolio A's $2 dividend). On the other hand, Portfolio B's stock appreciation gain is less than Portfolio A's because its stock is going up by only 5% (i.e., matching the smaller percentage dividend increase).

Portfolio B has the exact same total return (10%) each year as Portfolio A, but it is evenly balanced between cash dividend yield (5%) and market appreciation (5%). At the end of 10 years, Portfolio B earns the same cumulative total return as Portfolio A ($159) and its total portfolio value is the same ($259, which is its cumulative total return plus the $100 it started with), but it has reached there by a different route.

TABLE 4.2 Portfolio B: Dividend Growth Strategy (Equal Dividend and Growth)

Years	# of Shares at Start of Period	Share Price at Start of Period	Div. Rate (yield)	Div. Growth Rate	Div. Rate ($$) per Share	Next Year's Div. Rate	New Stock Price in Response to New Dividend Rate	This Year's Div. Income	This Year's Stock Price Increase Due to Dividend Increase	This Year's Total Return in $$$	This Year's Total Return %	# of New Shares Bought with Reinvested Dividend
1	1.00	100.00	5.0%	5.0%	5.00	5.25	105.00	5.00	5.00	10.00	10%	0.05
2	1.05	105.00	5.0%	5.0%	5.25	5.51	110.25	5.50	5.50	11.00	10%	0.05
3	1.10	110.25	5.0%	5.0%	5.51	5.79	115.76	6.05	6.05	12.10	10%	0.05
4	1.15	115.76	5.0%	5.0%	5.79	6.08	121.55	6.66	6.66	13.31	10%	0.05
5	1.20	121.55	5.0%	5.0%	6.08	6.38	127.63	7.32	7.32	14.64	10%	0.06
6	1.26	127.63	5.0%	5.0%	6.38	6.70	134.01	8.05	8.05	16.11	10%	0.06
7	1.32	134.01	5.0%	5.0%	6.70	7.04	140.71	8.86	8.86	17.72	10%	0.06
8	1.38	140.71	5.0%	5.0%	7.04	7.39	147.75	9.74	9.74	19.49	10%	0.07
9	1.45	147.75	5.0%	5.0%	7.39	7.76	155.13	10.72	10.72	21.44	10%	0.07
10	1.52	155.13	5.0%	5.0%	7.76	8.14	162.89	11.79	11.79	23.58	10%	0.07
Totals								79.69	79.69	159.37		

Exactly 50% of its total return has come from collecting and reinvesting cash dividends and the other 50% from market appreciation, matching precisely the 50-50 split between dividend yield (5%) and dividend growth (5%).

Portfolio C is our Income Factory portfolio where its single security has a market price of $100 and pays a dividend of $10, for a dividend yield of 10%. Like Portfolios A and B, Portfolio C earns a total return of 10%, but the entire return comes from the cash dividend, with no expectation of the dividend or stock price per share ever increasing. Going into the second year, Portfolio C's stock is paying the same dividend as before, so the only increase in portfolio income or value is due to the increasing number of shares Portfolio C owns as it reinvests its $10 dividend in new shares. With the biggest dividend to invest of all three portfolios, Portfolio C grows the number of shares it owns faster than the other two portfolios. On the other hand, it has no capital appreciation per share, with its 10% total return coming 100% from dividend income, reinvested to create its portfolio growth.

At the end of 10 years, Portfolio C, like the other two portfolios, has achieved a cumulative total return of $159 and has a total portfolio market value of $259. The only difference is that Portfolio C's accumulated return has been achieved solely through reinvestment and compounding of a dividend stream that has not grown at all on a per share basis.

The footnote below provides a link to a Seeking Alpha blog that contains a downloadable Excel spreadsheet for readers who wish to run their own numbers or projections with different yield or growth rate assumptions.*

---

* Copy this link into your browser or Google "Income Factory Update Blog": https://seekingalpha
.com/instablog/378031-steven-bavaria/5268938-income-factory-update-blog

TABLE 4.3 Portfolio C: Income Factory (High Yield/No Growth)

Years	# of Shares at Start of Period	Share Price at Start of Period	Div. Rate (yield)	Div. Growth Rate	Div. Rate ($$) per Share	Next Year's Div. Rate	New Stock Price in Response to New Dividend Rate	This Year's Div. Income	This Year's Stock Price Increase Due to Dividend Increase	This Year's Total Return in $$$	This Year's Total Return %	# of New Shares Bought with Reinvested Dividend
1	1.00	100.00	10.0%	0.0%	10.00	10.00	100.00	10.00	0.00	10.00	10%	0.10
2	1.10	100.00	10.0%	0.0%	10.00	10.00	100.00	11.00	0.00	11.00	10%	0.11
3	1.21	100.00	10.0%	0.0%	10.00	10.00	100.00	12.10	0.00	12.10	10%	0.12
4	1.33	100.00	10.0%	0.0%	10.00	10.00	100.00	13.31	0.00	13.31	10%	0.13
5	1.46	100.00	10.0%	0.0%	10.00	10.00	100.00	14.64	0.00	14.64	10%	0.15
6	1.61	100.00	10.0%	0.0%	10.00	10.00	100.00	16.11	0.00	16.11	10%	0.16
7	1.77	100.00	10.0%	0.0%	10.00	10.00	100.00	17.72	0.00	17.72	10%	0.18
8	1.95	100.00	10.0%	0.0%	10.00	10.00	100.00	19.49	0.00	19.49	10%	0.19
9	2.14	100.00	10.0%	0.0%	10.00	10.00	100.00	21.44	0.00	21.44	10%	0.21
10	2.36	100.00	10.0%	0.0%	10.00	10.00	100.00	23.58	0.00	23.58	10%	0.24
Totals								159.37	0.00	159.37		

53

Okay, the Math Works;
What About the Risks?

Most critics of the Income Factory eventually accept the fact that the math works and that two identical total returns, no matter how achieved, ultimately reach the same investment goals and accumulate the same amount of wealth. That usually turns the discussion to one about the risks involved. In particular, how do the risks of an Income Factory strategy compare to those of a traditional growth-oriented total return strategy?

The Income Factory's main risk is that the stocks or securities might fail to pay their dividends or distributions. That would be a major failure since the entire return on the investment is dependent on receiving and reinvesting those dividends or distributions. One obvious way to mitigate this risk is through broad diversification among individual stocks or funds, asset classes, and even portfolio managers. Asset class selection is critical, since high yields carry different risk profiles depending on what type of asset is paying them. As we discuss in more detail later on, the same yield level may be abnormally high and be a signal of significant risk in some asset classes, and yet be more mainstream and, therefore, not a sign of an unusually high risk level in others, depending on whether it represents equity or debt, where it ranks on the balance sheet, the structure of the investment vehicle, and other factors.

The major risk to a traditional total return strategy that depends on long-term steady dividend growth, is that a company's earnings slow down and its dividends don't grow as expected. With dividend yields typically only 2% or 3%, merely keeping up the current rate without growth would leave investors with a substandard return. Here again, diversification is the best way to mitigate this risk. Even if dividend champions were to stumble occasionally and not meet expectations, it is unlikely an entire portfolio of them would do so at the same time.

Another risk that both Income Factory and traditional total-return investors face is a major across-the-board economic downturn or bear market, that affects a company's stock and/or its underlying business temporarily, no matter how strong it may be otherwise. In this case both the Income Factory and traditional investors may see their portfolios drop in price and experience paper losses, as well as some drop in dividend income in the case of an economic downturn. The paper losses only become real (i.e., economic) losses if and when the investors sell out their positions.

Income Factory investors, because they are collecting cash at a high rate (8% to 10% or so) that they can reinvest and compound through the downturn, feel less pressure to do something—go to cash, sell off some assets, consider various hedging strategies (if it's not too late)—than traditional investors whose portfolios may be dead in the water and generating no growth (probably even losses) and not much cash. So the risk of a traditional growth investor bailing out and turning paper losses into real ones, thus forfeiting many of the benefits of their long-term investment strategy, is greater than the chance of that happening to the Income Factory investor.

In fact, many Income Factory investors embrace market downturns as opportunities to build their income stream faster than ever by reinvesting cash distributions at bargain prices and higher-than-normal yields, rather than fearing them as traditional total return investors do. For them, sitting on a river of cash that can be constantly reinvested to build their income stream has shifted the psychological dynamics of bear markets and other periods of turbulence. As an owner of an Income Factory with a long-term view, we can begin to see market downturns as opportunities to buy additional machines for our factory at rock-bottom prices.

Check Your Portfolio: You May Already Have an Income Factory

As suggested earlier, Income Factory investing is as much a state of mind as it is about selecting specific securities. Traditional investors with portfolios similar to Portfolio B earlier, more weighted toward current dividends and less dependent on future growth (e.g., 5% or even 6% dividend yields and only 4% or 5% dividend growth expectations), may already have portfolios with many characteristics of an Income Factory portfolio. The key is fully realizing that your portfolio's ability to steadily grow its cash output through all kinds of market environments makes you somewhat immune to the sort of market angst that plagues so many traditional equity investors.

So someone who has a portfolio that is collecting a solid 5% to 6% in dividends may not have an Income Factory, per se. Nor are they calling it that. But they are partway there and already capable of enjoying many of the benefits. I say "capable of" because it depends on whether they have an attitude that allows them to enjoy the benefits of owning a portfolio that is partially immune to market turbulence, or not.

Here is an example. I have a friend who had some long-term money to invest for his retirement, and after discussing his needs and expectations, I helped him pick out some solid utility and infrastructure stocks and funds that pay him dividends in the 6% to 7% range. He has owned them for several years and collects and reinvests the dividends steadily. But every few months he contacts me and says something like, "My friends all tell me the stock market is about to tank and I should sell out. What should I do?"

Then we invariably have the same conversation we did a few months earlier. I ask him, "Do you still own those stocks we bought? Are you still collecting your dividends every month and buying new shares with them?" Usually within a minute or two, I have "talked him off the ledge" and he admits that everything is going along just as he originally hoped when he made the investment a couple years earlier, regardless of what the market is doing.

My friend is a good example of somebody who basically has an Income Factory but doesn't fully realize it or enjoy the psychological benefit of it. He doesn't realize that his income is safe and growing even if the market is tanking, at least until it is pointed out to him. He hasn't yet internalized the fact that market turbulence is less threatening if he has a portfolio paying him 6% or more in cash dividends while prices are dropping, than if it is paying him only 2% or 3%, or even less.

The ultimate hedge against the macro risk of a bear market or sustained market drop is the ability and willingness to wait the market out because you are holding solid, dividend-paying stocks or other high-yielding securities, and accumulating more all the time by reinvesting your generous dividends. My friend has been experiencing the *financial* benefit of such a strategy, but has obviously been missing out on much of the *psychological* and *emotional* benefit of it, at least until it is pointed out to him.

Investors who eventually "get it" not only can enjoy all three benefits—psychological, emotional, and financial—but also realize that these three benefits are self-supportive and reinforcing. The psychological and emotional peace the Income Factory state of mind delivers can help us avoid making panicky decisions under stress. This helps ensure we get to enjoy the financial benefits, and to experience markets dropping and the invariable media stories of "the sky is falling" variety with greater equanimity, secure in the knowledge that our river of cash is flowing continuously and growing steadily.

For many investors these benefits may seem intuitive, but it is also worthwhile quantifying it mathematically so both our left brains and right brains are satisfied with the strategy we embrace. Under the Rule of 72 mentioned in Chapter 3, an income stream yielding 2% will require 36 years—more than a third of a lifetime—to double in value if it is reinvested and compounded. Even if, during the period of market turbulence or stagnation, the 2% yielding portfolio manages to grow its yield to 2.5% or 3%, at the new rates, it will still take 29 years or 24 years, respectively, to double itself. Nobody would expect to build a retirement income at that rate of growth. Given that reality—that is, a nongrowth or falling price environment—it may actually be a somewhat rational response for an investor to be stressed and feel that perhaps they needed to do something to change course or try to remedy the situation. Unfortunately at that point it is usually too late, although that still hasn't deterred millions of investors from selling out at what turn out in retrospect to be low points in market cycles, locking in losses and missed opportunities for years to come.

By comparison, a portfolio yielding 6% doubles and redoubles itself every 12 years. While not as much growth as one would ideally like (or as much as we expect our Income Factory to achieve), it is still a reasonable rate, especially if returns only remain that low for a few years before the market recovers. Think of two investors, one with the 2% yielding portfolio of growth-dependent dividend stocks, and the other with the 6% yielding portfolio, both facing an unknown but possibly prolonged period of market drop or turbulence. The first investor may be worried that if the market doesn't turn around quickly, they are stuck with an investment that is dropping or going nowhere while producing very little income. The second investor may still be concerned about the market turbulence, but knows if worse comes to worst, the cash income alone accounts for about two-thirds of an expected equity return. That should make it much easier for the second investor to "keep the faith" and stay in the market until it recovers.

The risks for both investors are quite different. The first investor takes the risk that (1) the companies whose stocks they hold in their portfolio may not manage to grow their earnings and dividends at the high rate they have in the past, or (2) even if they do, the market may ignore it. The second investor has less at stake if their stocks fail to grow their dividends, since they are not so dependent on dividend growth, but they do have to worry about possible dividend cuts or reductions. Both investors can mitigate some of these risks by diversification, including indexing. Neither can eliminate the risk of being caught in a severe market reversal, but it is less worrisome and scary for the second investor who can collect sizable dividends while waiting for the eventual correction.

That means the second investor is in a better position to turn off CNBC, take a deep breath, and wait out the storm, knowing that even if the market stays depressed for a while, the economic value of his or her portfolio is growing due to its sizable dividend stream. The first investor, without the cushion of a high cash dividend, may probably have a harder time staying the course, even if they realize— intellectually—that they are better off doing so.

That is how I became an Income Factory investor. Once I started shifting from traditional high-yielding equities (yields in the 5% to 6% range) to even higher-yielding asset classes that routinely paid in the 8% to 10% range, I realized that I didn't worry much about market price movements because my income was growing at an equity return rate regardless of what market prices did. Only a bit later did I realize that the story was even better, and that my income grew faster when markets were dropping than when they were rising, because I could reinvest and compound my dividends buying stocks that were "on sale."

Anyone thinking of adopting an Income Factory strategy would be wise to check their existing portfolio to see how much of a "factory" they already have. If you find a number of stocks or funds that pay yields of almost 6% or more, then you already have the nucleus of your Income Factory.

Income Factory Light Anyone?

At that point, an investor with a portfolio yielding about 6% might decide they have the best of both worlds and don't need to go all the way to a full, "income-only" Income Factory. That assumes their 6% yielding stocks also have the expectation of growing their dividends by 3% or 4% per year to achieve the full 8% or 10% equity return we all aspire to. If that is the case, and the 6% yield is enough of a cash hedge to give them the confidence needed to hold fast and not bail out during market downturns, then an Income Factory Light (IFL) strategy may fit the bill perfectly for them.

The essence of the Income Factory strategy is to be confident that if your cash income stream was all you got for some period of time, you could live with that (financially and psychologically) and hold tight indefinitely. For many of us, investing in securities that yield such a high rate that we get all the return we need to meet our goals in cash gives us the maximum insulation from market turbulence. But for investors who want to hedge their bets and collect a sizable portion of their total target return in cash (i.e., 6% or so) and still rely on the market to provide some of the growth, an Income Factory Light strategy provides an attractive alternative.

The portfolio choices for an IFL strategy would be broader than those available to a pure Income Factory investor. An Income Factory investor would want a portfolio that yields an average of 8% to 10% if they are targeting no stock price growth at all and therefore need to get their total equity return from cash dividends and distributions. That means they are probably looking to high-yield bonds and loans, business development companies (BDCs), master limited partnerships (MLPs), closed-end funds, exchange-traded funds (ETFs), and other alternative and/or higher-yielding securities that are structured and designed to maximize income to investors, with typically little or no growth expected at all.

IFL investors can consider all those asset classes. But since they are not depending exclusively on the cash yield for their total return, they can also continue to invest in the sort of slower-growing but higher-yielding stocks (e.g., utilities, real estate, etc.) that fall midway between a typical dividend growth stock and the high-yield assets that an Income Factory would target.

Income Factory: An Attitude, as Much as a Portfolio

It should be obvious by now that the concept of an Income Factory is a flexible one, intended to broaden the imagination of investors to not feel constrained by traditional norms or media-driven investment models that inhibit us from pursuing strategies tailored to our own investment goals. Central to that is the idea that building income for the long term is "Job 1," not chasing market prices that may or may not reflect our portfolio's real economic value. Doing that, for Income Factory adherents, involves buying high-yield and even ultra-high-yield securities whose cash distributions will provide our entire total return, indefinitely. But not every Income Factory advocate has to be a zealot (like myself), and there are numerous ways to build an IFL portfolio that (1) delivers enough current cash income to give the investor the confidence they need to keep the faith through market turbulence and downturns, while (2) also providing some expectation of upward growth in dividends, earnings, and stock prices during more robust market periods.

In later chapters, we provide a range of model portfolios for Income Factory and IFL investors, as well as links to an on-line site that updates the portfolios regularly. We also discuss in more detail some of the specific asset classes—including risks, rewards, and other features—that may be appropriate for both Income Factory and IFL portfolios.

What Sort of Income Factory Is Right for You?

Up until now we have focused on several main topics: (1) Why we believe it is the *income* our investment portfolios produce that reflects their real economic value, and in turn, ultimately determines their market value; (2) how the mathematical calculation of an investor's "total return" is completely indifferent to whether that return comes from cash payments received (dividends, etc.), or from share price growth or decline, or from both; (3) why focusing on building the income stream from our portfolio, rather than fixating on its ever-changing market value, can lead to greater peace of mind and more thoughtful investment decisions; and therefore, (4) why an Income Factory strategy that emphasizes current cash payments as the primary or even the exclusive source of long-term total return is an effective alternative strategy for many investors.

In this chapter we begin to turn our attention away from the theoretical and more toward the practical aspects of designing an Income Factory that fits our own personal needs. This means considering our financial goals, investment style, risk tolerance and comfort level, and tax situation, among other factors.

*   *   *

If you are still reading at this point, we assume you probably agree with or are at least open-minded about much of what you've read so far. So we turn our attention in this chapter to the nuts-and-bolts issues of how to go about designing and implementing an Income Factory strategy that matches our own needs, comfort level, and investing style. We saw in the last chapter that there can be various types of Income Factories, including even an Income Factory Light (IFL) for those who aren't ready to give up entirely their traditional dividend growth stocks.

So we review some of the factors to be considered in determining whether an Income Factory is appropriate for a particular investor, and if so, what design features it should ideally have. Here is a checklist of the key factors investors might consider in making those decisions:

- Your financial goals and investment perspective, including your age in relation to retirement (if that is your investment goal), or otherwise how soon do you need to start spending the money?
- Your attitude toward investing; are you more of a trader than an investor? Do you believe you can beat the market and enjoy the challenge? Do you relish the ups and downs and see them as opportunities to trade in and out and make money? Or would you prefer a smoother, less exciting ride?
- Your personal risk/reward comfort level (What is your "risk tolerance"?)
- Your tax status (Will your Income Factory be held in a tax-deferred account, like an IRA, or in a taxable account?)
- Your familiarity with various types of securities and asset classes, and your sense of adventure about considering alternative asset classes beyond the usual suspects.

There are appropriate Income Factories for almost everyone, depending on their opinions, feelings, and attitudes about the preceding issues, which we discuss in greater detail. Our goal is to help you select, design, and create the right one.

Financial Goals and Timing

Income Factories are about using the power of compounding cash and the Rule of 72 to relentlessly grow your income over the long term. That means they are perfect vehicles for people who are investing for a retirement that is still many decades off into the future, or for people who may be closer to retirement or even in their early retirement years but realize they most likely require that income stream for another 20 years or so and need to continue investing with a long-term outlook.

Many people in their 60s or even 70s think that they need to change their investment strategies once they hit retirement. In some cases they do. One example would be if they are invested in a traditional high-growth/low-yield equity strategy that requires them to sell off and liquidate principal in their portfolio to generate the income they need to live on. It can be very stressful for people if they know they are going to have to sell off a certain portion of their portfolio every month, regardless of whether market prices are up or down. They would never know in advance if they were going to be forced to liquidate assets at a market low point. Then they might be kicking themselves a month or so later if the market comes back up and they realize they have invaded their permanent capital more than they originally projected in their financial plans, or more than would have been necessary if they had only waited a bit.

But if they had begun using an Income Factory strategy before retiring, then they would already have been collecting a high level of cash each month and would not have had to invade their capital. Once they retire, instead of reinvesting and compounding their *entire* river of cash as they had been doing in their preretirement growth stage, all they would have to do post-retirement is distribute a portion of their income stream to themselves to cover living expenses, while keeping the remainder in the Income Factory where they could continue to reinvest it. Thus, even after retirement they would still be able to keep on growing their Income Factory output, albeit at a slower rate than previously when they could reinvest the entire income stream.

It should be obvious that an Income Factory strategy is equally appropriate for any investor seeking to build long-term wealth, even when the purpose is not related to their anticipated retirement. The key qualities an Income Factory investor requires are (1) a willingness to regard income as the essential element and measure of a portfolio's *economic* value, and (2) the patience to let that economic value accumulate, in the form of constantly increasing income growth, without getting overly anxious even when the market fails to consistently reflect that economic value in the price of the portfolio generating it.

This last point is critical. It would be fair to suggest that an Income Factory investor is making a leap of faith in believing Mr. Market is rational enough over the long term that it will ultimately recognize the economic value of a continually growing income stream and incorporate it into the price of the securities producing that income. But even if Mr. Market fails to do that, or delays doing it indefinitely, Income Factory investors know they are getting the *economic* value they really care about over the long term, that is, the ever-growing river of cash.

Those with shorter time horizons need to think carefully about what sort of investment strategy is appropriate for meeting their goals. Someone with small children or just starting a family who is planning how to invest for college expenses 15 or 20 years out might very well decide that a long-term strategy is appropriate. But they would want to be sure to begin ramping it down in terms of risk and potential volatility as they got closer to the time when they knew the funds would be needed.

"Ramping it down" might mean discontinuing the reinvestment of dividends four or five years before expenditures are required, and letting the funds accumulate in more liquid form, like a short-term government or corporate bond fund, a money market fund, or even bank CDs, depending on the investor's individual preferences and comfort level. It might also mean gradually moving the entire portfolio into less volatile asset classes, like those just mentioned.

Of course, those who are saving for a shorter-term purpose, like purchasing a car or the down payment on a home, have no reason to consider an Income Factory or any other sort of long-term investment strategy that involves price volatility or illiquidity risk. They should maintain their assets in more stable, liquid securities where they don't run the risk of needing to cash out and spend their money just as the market is in decline.

Personal Attitudes: Investor or Trader?

We said in the last chapter that an Income Factory is an attitude toward investing, as much as it is a portfolio strategy. By maximizing the current cash we collect in dividends or distributions, and seeking to earn our entire equity return up front, in cash, we are also settling for a long-term return of "only" 8% or 10%, or whatever high-yield benchmark we set for ourselves. Now to me, and to most investors, the prospect of achieving a long-term annual equity return in the range of 8% to 10% seems quite attractive. But plenty of investors believe they can beat the long-term averages and do better than that, either by astute stock picking, or shrewd trading techniques, or the skillful use of hedges, options, and other trading tools and derivatives.

Aggressive traders and investors with that level of confidence might view the strategies that Income Factory investors use to ensure long-term steady income growth as an encumbrance, a drag on their ability to score above-average market gains. Most traders and active stock pickers believe not only that they can beat the averages, but for the great majority of them, that what they do is challenging, exciting, and even fun. So for most of them, an Income Factory or other long-term buy-and-hold strategy would probably not be a particularly appropriate (or even satisfying) choice. At least not in the short term. It might be satisfying in the long run, however, since most investors who think they can beat the market averages obviously fail to do so, and might wish—later on—that they had employed a more predictable, "steady Eddie" sort of strategy.

There is a reason why CNBC, Bloomberg, and Fox Business News organize their round-the-clock coverage of the financial markets in the same the way ESPN does its sports coverage. They have trained millions of viewers and investors to believe that tracking stock market prices, economic data releases, and other activities and events that appear to influence financial markets is a critical part of investing. It is an attractive, even addictive, message and has turned investing and the financial markets generally, in the eyes of many, into a sort of sporting or entertainment event that demands constant attention.

In the interest of full disclosure, I have to admit that despite having written dozens of articles (and now even this book) extolling the merits of taking a long-term view that focuses on the income and ignores short-term market price movements, I still check the prices of the securities in my Income Factory virtually every day. We may know that the income is what counts and that market declines even make our income grow faster as we reinvest at bargain prices, but there is still something visceral about needing to follow our portfolio's daily market value and preferring to see our stocks rise in price, despite that being counterintuitive to our professed strategy.

So there may be a bit of the trader mentality in all of us, despite our being firmly committed intellectually and strategically to a long-term Income Factory approach. This is something to keep in mind as we design and then manage our own Income Factory portfolios. We shall see that it is possible to create an Income Factory that requires very little monitoring, with the sort of "buy 'em and forget 'em" stocks and funds that you could ignore for long periods of time and they still accumulate, reinvest, compound, and grow their income streams just fine. You could even leave instructions with your brokerage firm to reinvest the dividends automatically and have a truly automated Income Factory that would probably perform about as well as one that was more actively managed.

Personally, for me, that would be too much like "watching paint dry" and I need to be more active. So I review my portfolio regularly, continually reinvesting dividends opportunistically in securities that currently look attractive, while also tweaking the portfolio periodically by selling funds and stocks that have appreciated and reallocating to assets that have not done so well price-wise and now appear to be bargains.

So there is plenty of opportunity within an overall Income Factory approach to indulge our inner trader without sacrificing the long-term benefits of the strategy. Of course, if one opts for an IFL strategy, mixing and matching high-yielding no-growth fixed income assets with more modest-yielding dividend growth stocks, then there may be even greater opportunity for portfolio tweaking and rebalancing.

Sleeping Well at Night
(a.k.a. "Risk Tolerance")

Risk tolerance is the amount of variability in the return that investors are comfortable accepting in their investment portfolios. It is an important aspect in selecting an investing strategy because our capacity and willingness to endure swings (large or small) in the value of our investments typically determines whether we hold fast during turbulent periods, or panic and sell at inopportune times. In some ways risk tolerance is related to the "personal attitude" discussion earlier, where we compared the trader and investor mentalities and concluded that some of us have a bit of both, even if we are intellectually committed to a long-term buy-and-hold strategy.

But risk tolerance and investment style are not the same thing. Just because some investors love to trade actively or take aggressive positions in risky growth stocks does not necessarily mean they have the requisite nerves of steel and emotional and psychological toughness to handle the market ups and downs that such a strategy might require. Although some of them do, many traders and active investors find out when the pressure is on and they see markets starting to move precipitously that they don't have the power of their convictions or the staying power they may have once thought they did. It is this tendency of many investors—across the spectrum from traders to more conservative ones—to panic when markets tank or hit rough patches, and head for the hills and sell out, that often exacerbates what would otherwise be routine cyclical downturns and random market declines.

It is this realization, that broad swings in investor sentiment are (1) just as common among traders and more "sophisticated" investors as among ordinary retail investors, and (2) often not connected with economic reality, that helps motivate many investors to seek out alternative strategies, like the Income Factory, that are not so tethered to or dependent upon market price movements. But even among the potential long-term buy-and-hold investors who are the target population for the Income Factory strategy, there is still a broad spectrum of risk tolerance and comfort levels.

In theory, Income Factory adherents have already embraced the idea that income distributions are paramount and short-term market price movements are less relevant. But that doesn't mean we have eliminated risks. What it means essentially is that we have replaced the risk that most stock market investors and media commentators fixate upon—the risk of market prices falling—with a different risk: the risk of our income stream declining or disappearing. This would likely happen in one or another of the following ways:

- Companies whose stock we own can cut or eliminate their dividend payments
- Companies whose loans or bonds we own can fail to make their principal and interest payments
- Funds we own can cut their distributions, usually because the underlying stocks, bonds, or loans they hold have cut back or missed their own dividends, principal, or interest payments

The risk of individual companies failing to either pay their debts or earn enough to make their dividend payments is probably the most common, generic sort of investment risk there is. It is hard to protect against, no matter how much analysis and due diligence we do on the particular companies, because lightning of some sort (business

reversals, bad decisions, fraud, dramatic shifts in technology or con-
sumer tastes, etc.) can strike anytime or anyplace.

Fortunately, individual entity risk at an overall portfolio level is
fairly avoidable, if we practice diversification. So rule one, whether
employing an Income Factory strategy or a conventional dividend
growth or total return strategy, is *diversify*. In my own investing, I
practice this mostly by investing in mutual funds (generally closed-
end funds, but we discuss that later since my reasons for that go well
beyond diversification) or occasionally, exchange-traded funds (ETFs)
or exchange-traded notes (ETNs).

Diversifying and holding funds rather than individual company
stocks or bonds obviously helps minimize the risk of our entire portfolio's cash flow being severely impacted if a single company or small
number of companies were to cut their dividends. But there is still a
danger to our cash flow if some macro-economic trend or industry-
wide event were to disrupt the dividend-paying capacity of a particular
fund, despite its holding a diversified portfolio of assets.

For this reason, we want our Income Factory to hold a broad, diversified assortment of funds representing various industries and asset
classes, so the same disruptive macro-economic event or trend would
likely not affect all of them in the same way. These industries and asset
classes might include:

- Corporate stock funds of all kinds—general or specialized
  by industry, like real estate, utilities, finance, energy, business
  development companies (BDCs), etc.
- Corporate bond funds—in our case, mostly high-yield bond
  funds (*high-yield* meaning bonds issued by companies rated
  "non-investment grade" or below the rating level of triple-B-
  minus; in other words, most companies, since the great majority
  of all companies are non-investment grade)
- Corporate loan funds—loans to the same cohort of companies,
  except loans are less risky than bonds (even bonds issued by
  the same company), because loans (1) are higher up the balance sheet (i.e., they get paid first and are usually secured by

corporate assets) and (2) are floating-rate (i.e., there is little or
no interest rate risk)

- "Structured" asset classes—funds that hold specific asset types
  like corporate loans and bonds, home mortgages, auto loans,
  and so on that are "securitized" (i.e., pooled into special-
  purpose vehicles that are leveraged multiple times, creating
  greater risk and return for investors) and typically designed to
  provide high current income
- Other specialized asset classes, like preferred stocks, convertible
  securities, master limited partnerships (MLPs), and so on

We discuss some of these asset classes and vehicles for holding them
later on, but for now the main idea to emphasize is that we want broad
diversification in the underlying companies whose performance we
are betting on, and also in the types of instruments (stocks, bonds,
structured vehicles, etc.) that we are holding and the types of industries that we are exposed to. In addition, I like diversification among
investment managers as well, since managers often have their own
investing styles and views about the economy, the industry, and/or
the asset class in which they invest. So even within a particular investment category (e.g., real estate funds, high-yield bond funds), I prefer
to own more than one fund and fund manager.

One way to visualize what we are doing is to imagine our Income
Factory output as a river of cash that we are collecting constantly
each month or quarter, depending on our funds' payment schedules,
and that we want our sources of that cash to be literally thousands of
smaller rivers and tributaries feeding into our Income Factory from
all throughout our global economy. Each little river or tributary, in
turn, is actually a company whose management team has "skin in
the game"—that is, their jobs, their salaries, their bonuses, their stock
and stock options—and is working constantly to keep their company
afloat, growing it, paying its bills, growing its dividends, and so on.

So when we consider the risk we are taking in our factory and what
sort of risk level we can personally tolerate, we are actually assessing
how comfortable we are with the particular network of tributaries and

rivers feeding into our factory. Some rivers are very steady, with a consistent, unbroken history at a modest level of flow, while others are faster and more turbulent, with a higher level of flow.

We can design an Income Factory at either end of that spectrum, one targeting a higher cash yield and longer term return, but with a greater risk of volatility and variation along the way; another targeting a somewhat lower return but less excitement and perhaps a smoother ride.

Later on, we have some chapters outlining model portfolios reflecting different Income Factory strategies and risk levels. In general, the higher a security's yield, the riskier it is. That reflects what is pretty intuitive, that Mr. Market demands to be paid more for taking a higher risk than for taking a lower risk. So a security paying a 10% yield should, "in general" (a major caveat, by the way), represent more risk to the investor than a security paying, say, 6%.

Choosing Which Risks to Worry About

But not all risks are the same. The risks we are worried about are the risks to our income stream—that is, the dividends and distributions that provide the river of cash that is our Income Factory output. But some of the additional yield that Mr. Market requires from certain securities represents risks that may not concern us. For example, some of the risk may represent *liquidity risk*. Liquidity risk relates to the perceived lack of instant marketability of an investment. Securities issued by smaller companies, or bought and sold in smaller markets with less volume, may be more difficult for investors to sell and get their money out of quickly, especially during market declines or periods of volatility. That is a big deal for many investors, especially institutions that have to mark their portfolios to market at the end of every day, and therefore it is reasonable the market would price less liquid or illiquid securities to yield more than securities regarded as equivalent risks in other respects.

The same is true for certain types of funds. Closed-end funds, because investors cannot go to the fund management company any day they want and demand that it redeem their shares at their net asset value (as they can with traditional open-end funds), have to pay higher distribution yields than typical mutual funds to attract investors. For Income Factory investors, who are focused on the long-term investing and compounding of our portfolio income, this additional liquidity risk is of little concern. That is because we are seldom under pressure to sell particular securities in our portfolio on a specific day or at a specific time. So we are mostly content to accept the additional yield for taking a risk we don't really regard as all that risky within our investment strategy.

Now if we had a *different* investment strategy, one that required us to do a lot of split-second, in-and-out trading, or to trade in large institutional block volumes, then liquidity and the ability to buy and sell in a highly transparent and efficient market would be very important to us. Similarly, if we were an institutional fund manager who had to report and defend our investment results to corporate clients, and mark-to-market our portfolio on a daily or weekly basis, then we would be quite concerned about liquidity risk. As retail investors, whose only client we have to satisfy is ourselves, we can ignore illiquidity concerns and worries about paper losses that would constrain larger institutional players.

Complexity Risk

Another risk that we can get paid extra for taking but without having to lose sleep over (if we do our homework and are careful), is what I put under the general heading of "complexity risk." Complexity risk reflects the additional structural complications or unusual features of a security that require extra due diligence on the part of the investor to understand and feel comfortable with. Just as asset classes that involve more liquidity risk generally command a higher yield than more liquid securities, the same is true of securities that involve greater complexity risk.

This merely reflects the law of supply and demand at work in the financial markets. If a security is less liquid than some other securities, then there are fewer investors willing to buy it and the market has to set the price a bit lower and the dividend yield higher to induce those investors who are open-minded about buying it to do so. Similarly with complexity risk, if a security is more complicated to understand and takes more due diligence on the part of investors to feel comfortable with having it in their portfolios, that discourages some investors and they choose not to buy it. That lowers the demand for it, so once again the market price has to be lower and the cash yield a bit higher than it otherwise would be to induce investors to buy it and thus, as economists would say, "clear the market."

The reality is, a number of very attractive asset classes carry a complexity risk premium, where investors willing to do the additional due diligence required to understand the securities can be paid well for going to the extra trouble. Among these are funds that invest in "structured portfolios" of corporate loans, which are called collateralized loan obligations (CLOs). CLOs have been around for several decades and are essentially "virtual" commercial banks, where the sponsor purchases a portfolio of senior secured corporate loans, originally underwritten by major banks. The sponsor funds the investment by borrowing about 90% of the required funds and putting up equity of the remaining 10%, replicating pretty closely the capital structure of a commercial bank, but without the bricks and mortar and large staff. CLOs, overall, have the distinction of having come through the great crash of 2008 successfully, rewarding their equity investors handsomely and demonstrating to later investors (like us) the durability of their structure. Readers see that we have several CLO funds in our model portfolios, listed later on. (Caveat: Names can be important. CLOs have a very similar name and acronym to collateralized *debt* obligations [CDOs], which were the securitized vehicles created to hold what proved to be substandard home mortgages and home equity loans in the early 2000s. Many of these were ultimately toxic and helped trigger the great crash of 2008. Some reporters and commentators still confuse the toxic CDOs with the benign, well-behaved CLOs. Investors should be careful not to fall for the occasional scare article about CLOs where a journalist has confused the two asset classes.)

CLOs are just one of the asset classes that may be unknown to many retail investors, but are worth learning about if we want to boost our Income Factory output without taking on more risk than is reasonable. Other assets that pay higher cash yields than they probably would if they were less complex and easier for the average investor to figure out are MLPs. MLPs are used mostly for investments in the oil and gas industry, transportation, storage and infrastructure, and other assets that generate long-tailed, predictable cash flows. CLOs and MLPs are just two of the more obvious complex assets that we consider for our Income Factory. These and many other complex assets are somewhat harder to understand than ordinary, straightforward stocks and bonds, but they generally are worth going to the extra trouble to do so. Moreover, we can lessen and diffuse both complexity and liquidity risk through (1) holding them in diversified funds, not by buying individual securities, and (2) choosing experienced, professional fund managers.

Credit Risk

Finally, the other risk that we generally get paid higher cash yields for taking than we do for accepting normal equity risk is credit risk. That may surprise some readers, since one's reaction might be, "Credit risk? We all know about credit risk. Don't you get paid *less* for taking credit risk than for taking equity risk (i.e., for buying the stock)?" The answer is yes, in theory, you should get paid more for taking the equity risk than for taking the credit risk. After all, taking the equity risk (i.e., being a stockholder) does involve taking more risk than taking the credit risk (i.e., buying the loans or bonds). If you buy the equity, the company has to do two things: (1) at a minimum, stay alive and pay all its debts and other obligations, and (2) expand and grow its business, its earnings, and—ultimately—its dividends.

If you buy its credit, the company has to do only one thing: stay alive and pay its debts (interest and principal). As a creditor, you don't care whether the company thrives, only that it survives. If it does that, creditors receive all their interest and principal, even if the company never grows its earnings at all and stockholders never make a dime.

So given the additional risk stockholders take, they should—if markets are rational and efficient—make a greater return than creditors over the long run. But in the short term, in terms of current cash payments—that is, dividends for stockholders, interest for loan and bond investors—it is reasonable that the debt investors would get more up front. After all, their interest and principal payments are all they are going to get, ever, regardless of how well the company ultimately does in the future. Stockholders are expected to be content with less cash upfront precisely because they get their reward later on when (and if) the increased earnings and dividends start to roll in.

That's the theory. But we saw a couple chapters ago how complicated and potentially time-consuming the process can be for Mr. Market to recognize a company's business success and then incorporate it into the price of its stock. That is especially so if the market as a whole has other ideas and is moving sideways or declining, even if the fundamentals of the overall economy or of individual companies suggest—in theory—it should be moving in the opposite direction.

That's why I have previously written that equity investing involves a lot of "wishing, waiting, and hoping" (i.e., for the earnings, dividend, and stock price growth to materialize later on), whereas fixed income investing involves getting your entire return—or at least most of it— paid up front in cash payments. The risk/reward choice an investor has in this case is clear. A predictable return of perhaps 6% or 8% in current cash payments (or more if bought in a closed-end fund), with little expectation of achieving any more than that, or a lower current cash payment of only 3% or 4%, with the promise, expectation, or hope of more than that in the future if both the company and Mr. Market do what they are supposed to do.

Risk and Reward in a Nutshell

We get paid for taking risk. But not all risks are equally worrisome to every investor. If we want to maximize our potential return in building an Income Factory, we should try to identify the risks we want to really focus our attention on, as opposed to other risks that Mr. Market worries about and therefore pays us more to take but which, in fact, we are not so worried about. Let's summarize what we've discussed so far about risk and reward, and spell out its implications for Income Factory investors:

- Although market price risk is the principal risk most traditional investors worry about more than any other, as Income Factory investors we try to ignore it as much as possible.
- Instead, we focus on maximizing cash dividends and distributions, so the major risk we worry about is the possibility of dividend or distribution cuts that would disrupt our Income Factory's cash output.
- The individual company risk of a dividend or distribution cut is serious and cuts across all industries and asset classes; but fortunately it can largely be mitigated through diversification, which is why I use mutual funds and similar commingled vehicles.
- That still leaves three other risks that we discussed and investors must decide for themselves whether they are comfortable taking and whether they feel adequately compensated for doing so: liquidity risk, complexity risk, and credit risk.
- Often liquidity and complexity risk go together. Typically your less-liquid asset classes are also more complex, and vice versa. That's not surprising because it may be the greater complexity and additional due diligence required that reduces the potential investor base for certain asset classes, making them less liquid and driving up their distribution yields.
- Those investors who truly embrace the Income Factory philosophy and can learn to ignore the market price volatility of their most complex, least liquid securities, may find these to be their highest-yielding and most attractive performers.
- Investors who are less comfortable with that degree of illiquidity and complexity risk can still build an Income Factory with more conventional asset classes, but may give up a percent or two of additional distribution yield to do so.
- Investors who make that relatively lower-risk choice likely are populating their Income Factory with funds that hold more

widely known asset classes, including high-yielding stocks and fixed-income asset classes like high-yield bonds, corporate loans, preferred stocks, and convertible bonds.

■ Whether they opt for the higher-yielding and therefore higher risk/higher reward Income Factory, or a more moderate risk/ moderate reward version, the goal is the same: an income stream that relentlessly pumps out cash through all sorts of economic and market cycles, which can be reinvested to create constant growth of the Income Factory itself.

Taxes and Your Income Factory

My original Income Factory portfolio was and still is a traditional Individual Retirement Account (IRA) that I have been investing personally for over 30 years. IRAs, whether traditional IRAs or Roth IRAs, allow an investor to defer taxes, permanently for Roth IRAs and until distributions are taken for traditional IRAs. In either case, there are no current tax consequences during the life of the IRA, so you can trade in and out of specific securities, make capital gains, and collect and reinvest dividends and distributions, all without any tax consequences until you take distributions, which may be many decades later, depending on your age when you create the IRA. This makes IRAs the perfect vehicle for holding, reinvesting, and compounding high-dividend and high-distribution securities, since the entire "inside build-up" is tax deferred (or totally tax free if you do it within a Roth IRA).

This ability to defer current taxes is a valuable asset in itself, inasmuch as it allows us to grow an income stream at a much faster compounded rate within an IRA than the income stream from the exact same portfolio would be able to grow in a taxable account. Let us demonstrate this with a simple example.

Suppose you create an Income Factory that yields 10% within an IRA and you therefore reinvest and compound that 10% distribution, tax-deferred, over—let us assume—a 30-year period. Under our familiar rule of compounding, the Rule of 72, a 10% income stream doubles itself about every 7.2 years and becomes about 18 times what you started with at the end of 30 years.

Suppose, for comparison sake, you invested in a taxable account at 10% for 30 years. (To do that you might need "tax advantaged" and other tax-friendly closed-end funds like those listed in "Income Factory Model Portfolio—Taxable Account" in Table 9.3 in Chapter 9.) Let us assume your distributions were either "qualified" and taxed at the 15% rate that most investors have to pay on their dividend income (if their incomes are less than about $425,000, above which the qualified rate goes up to 20%) or were treated as return of capital and untaxed. That means the effective dividend yield at which you can reinvest and compound this portfolio is about 8.5%.

Compounding at that rate your Income Factory output would increase its output by about 12 times over 30 years. That is still a considerable achievement, but obviously the advantage of doing it within a tax-deferred IRA, where the same portfolio would increase by 18 times, is a significant advantage.

TABLE 5.1 Tale of Two Income Factories: IRA and Taxable Account
(Assume Each Factory Starts Out with Portfolios Earning $5,000 Annual Cash Income)

	IRA	Taxable Account
Gross Yield	10%	10%
Net Yield After Tax (If Applicable)	10%	8.5%
# of Years to Double When Compounded	7.2	8.5
Initial Cash Income	5,000	5,000
Doubles to $10,000 after:	7.2 years	8.5 years
Redoubles to $20,000 in:	14.4 years	17 years
Redoubles to $40,000 in:	21.6 years	25.5 years
Redoubles to $80,000 in:	28.8 years	34 years
Redoubles to $160,000 in:	36 years	42.5 years
Redoubles to $320,000 in:	43.2 years	51 years

Table 5.1, "Tale of Two Income Factories," summarizes this comparison, clearly showing what a difference an extra percentage point or two can add to your income stream over many years. Starting with identical portfolios each earning annual cash yields of $5,000, the untaxed IRA portfolio gets to reinvest and compound its full 10% earnings yield each year, so its $5,000 income grows to $80,000 per year in about 29 years. The Income Factory paying the 15% qualified dividend tax doesn't reach the $80,000 per year mark until 34 years, a full 5 years later than the untaxed IRA factory. Two years later, at year 36, the IRA has already redoubled its income again, to $160,000, while the taxed portfolio won't reach $160,000 until midway through its 42nd year, at which point the IRA is already almost up to twice that amount, or $320,000 per year.

This demonstrates, of course, the obvious advantages of reinvesting and compounding within a tax-advantaged vehicle. It also demonstrates the difference that one or two percentage points can make in our cumulative earnings over the long term, if we are disciplined about our reinvestment program. But just because an investor is not able to use an IRA or other tax-deferred vehicle for their Income Factory does not preclude them from using the strategy. As we have seen, being able to reinvest and compound 85% of one's cash income can still provide a substantial growth over time, even if the "leakage" to pay taxes reduces the river of cash from what it otherwise would be.

But asset class selection is critical, since some asset classes or investment vehicles are more taxpayer friendly than others, and therefore are better choices for a taxable Income Factory. With a tax-deferred Income Factory, like an IRA, we can hold almost any sort of asset we want, without respect to its tax qualities. That allows us to focus completely on its suitability as an income generator, balancing its yield, its safety, its risk/reward profile, and generally how comfortable we are with it in our own portfolio. In selecting assets for a taxable Income Factory, we need to consider all those things as well. But we also need to determine how much of the distribution is actually income as opposed to a return of capital, and then if it is income, we need to determine whether it is "qualified" dividend income or just plain ordinary income. In later chapters we include a taxable Income Factory model portfolio along with other model portfolios designed for IRAs or other tax-free or tax-deferred strategies.

In general, many of the highest yielding and therefore higher risk/reward investment opportunities will likely be most appropriate for IRAs and tax-deferred investors. That's because they use credit instruments (loans, bonds, and synthetic credit structures) whose distributions largely represent interest payments that—unlike stock dividends—are taxed at regular tax rates rather than the lower qualified dividend rate. On the other hand, some of these higher-yielding assets pay a portion of their distributions in the form of "return of capital," which is not taxed but merely reduces the investors' cost base, essentially deferring their tax indefinitely until they sell the asset. In that case, reinvesting and compounding those distributions (or at least the portion that is return of capital) serves to defer taxes, even in a taxable account, somewhat similarly to what happens within a traditional IRA.

Closed-end funds that invest in MLPs and real estate, both popular Income Factory asset choices, typically pay a portion of their distributions in the form of return of capital, which means they both might be candidates for taxable Income Factories. Similarly, many equity funds pay out a portion of their distributions as return of capital, and to that extent are not taxable. The taxable character of a fund's distributions can vary widely from one year to the next, between qualified (taxed at the lower rate), unqualified (taxed at higher, regular rates), and return of capital (untaxed, but possibly "constructive" or "destructive" and thus deserving of further analysis). Therefore, it is essential to look closely at the distribution history of each particular closed-end fund that one is considering to see what its record has been with regard to the tax character of its distributions before making a decision whether to include it or not.

Asset Classes: Beyond the "Usual Suspects"

By now we have discussed how an investor's (1) financial goals and timing, (2) attitude toward investing ("trader" or "investor"), (3) risk/

reward comfort level (risk tolerance), and (4) tax situation will all influence whether they are a candidate for an Income Factory strategy, and if so, what sort of Income Factory they select.

In my own investing experience, I evolved to what I later began to call the Income Factory over a period of about 10 years. At first, I invested in typical dividend growth stocks, like utilities, energy companies, and other large blue chips, collecting dividends in the 4% to 5% range and expecting (hoping) to get growth on top of that to bring me up to that historical average equity return of 8% to 10% that I had read about for much of my investing life. I also invested in typical mutual funds, again favoring those that focused on large, well-established dividend-paying companies. Then I began to discover other types of assets that routinely seemed to pay higher levels of cash dividends and distributions. Many of these were fixed-income securities of one sort or another—high-yield bonds, convertible bonds, preferred stocks—where you traded off the sort of future growth you got with stocks in return for higher cash yields in the present. I also discovered closed-end funds, which I came to understand and appreciate as ideal vehicles for owning less liquid and sometimes more complex high-yielding securities. As a result, closed-end funds have now become my personal investment vehicle of choice for my own Income Factory.

Each investor has to find the particular asset classes and investment vehicles they are most comfortable with for their own Income Factory. There may be some trade-offs. Traditional asset classes—like corporate stocks—that most investors are immediately familiar with may pay dividend yields too low to provide that river of cash we are looking for if our Income Factory output is going to be high enough to provide (1) the feeling of security we need to insulate us from market downturns as well as (2) the high rate of reinvestment and compounding we need to meet our long-term goals. Fortunately, we don't have to step very far out of a typical investor's comfort zone to find diversified portfolios of closed-end funds of many different asset types with solid records and distribution yields in the 7% to 10% range. We provide a core list of funds in Chapter 6 that would be good candidates for most

Income Factories. In Chapter 7 we take it a step further and present specific model portfolios for investors with various portfolio sizes and risk/reward comfort levels.

With that core list of fund candidates, and specific models drawn from that list, an investor has a number of options for starting their own Income Factory, including ways to personalize their strategy, if they choose to do so. The first option is to use one of the model portfolios. As we see later on when we present various model portfolios, a number of attractive Income Factories can be built with closed-end funds using traditional asset classes well-known to most investors (dividend-paying stocks, bonds, loans, convertible securities, preferred stocks) with a range of target distribution yields from lower risk/reward profile (7% to 8%) to higher risk/reward profile (9% to 10%). These would likely perform well from the standpoint of both (1) delivering the necessary river of cash to compound income and (2) providing the psychological and emotional edge needed to ride out market declines over time.

More adventurous investors can "soup up" their Income Factory by blending in some funds or asset classes with higher risk/reward profiles, and yields to match, like BDC funds, structured loan funds (also known as collateralized loan obligations, or CLOs), MLP funds, or leveraged ETFs or ETNs. Many of these funds or vehicles pay distributions yielding in the low double digits or occasionally higher, so adding even just a relatively small portion of them to our Income Factory's portfolio can have a considerable impact on our long-term earning, reinvestment, and compounding rate. For example, if you started with a portfolio having an average return of 9% and replaced 20% of it with assets averaging 12% yields, the overall portfolio average yield would increase to 9.6%, with the extra 6/10 of 1% making a considerable difference when compounded over the long term. (See Table 5.2.)

Those dividend-growth investors, or others who want to keep a portion of their portfolios in traditional corporate equities that pay modest dividends but offer an expectation of dividend and stock growth along with it, can blend that with an Income Factory and still enjoy some of the benefits of both. We described this earlier as

TABLE 5.2 Impact of "Souping Up" Our Income Factory

Shows How Adding Higher Risk/Reward Assets Affects Overall Yield of "Base" Income Factory

Yield of Base Income Factory	% of Higher-Yielding 12% Assets Added to Base	Yield of "Souped-Up" Income Factory
9.00%	0%	9.00%
9.00%	5%	9.15%
9.00%	10%	9.30%
9.00%	15%	9.45%
9.00%	20%	9.60%
9.00%	25%	9.75%
9.00%	30%	9.90%
9.00%	35%	10.05%
9.00%	40%	10.20%
9.00%	45%	10.35%
9.00%	50%	10.50%

(Yield on souped-up assets: 12%)

an Income Factory Light. For example, an investor who wants the income stability through "thick and thin" of an Income Factory, but still would prefer to exercise their inner trader and stock picker, might choose a blended strategy that was 75% Income Factory, yielding 9% and no expectation of growth, and 25% traditional dividend-growth stocks, yielding perhaps 3% with an expectation of another 6% or 7% growth. Table 5.3 indicates that such a combination would provide us with a blended portfolio yield of 7.5%, not enough cash, when reinvested and compounded, to provide us with our target Income Factory total return of 8% to 10%, but perhaps enough to provide the current cash required to stiffen the investor's spine during turbulent market periods. Ideally the 25% non–Income Factory portion of the portfolio would deliver, in addition to its 3% yield, enough growth to push the entire portfolio up by another couple percentage points into equity return territory.

Table 5.3 also shows some additional IFL combinations. An investor can vary both (1) the blend of Income Factory funds versus dividend growth stocks (e.g., 50/50, 75/25) as well as (2) the risk/reward profile of both the Income Factory portfolio (e.g., 9% target distribution, 10.5%, or 12%) and the dividend growth portfolio (e.g., 3% or 5% average yields).

TABLE 5.3 Various Income Factory Light Combinations

Percentage in Income Factory	Percentage in Dividend Growth Portfolio	Average Yield in IF	Average Yield in DG	Blended Portfolio Yield
75%	25%	9.0%	3.0%	7.5%
75%	25%	10.5%	3.0%	8.6%
75%	25%	12.0%	3.0%	9.8%
75%	25%	9.0%	5.0%	8.0%
75%	25%	10.5%	5.0%	9.1%
75%	25%	12.0%	5.0%	10.3%
50%	50%	9.0%	3.0%	6.0%
50%	50%	10.5%	3.0%	6.8%
50%	50%	12.0%	3.0%	7.5%
50%	50%	9.0%	5.0%	7.0%
50%	50%	10.5%	5.0%	7.8%
50%	50%	12.0%	5.0%	8.5%

The table shows only the yield of the resulting blended portfolios and does not include whatever additional total return might be expected from capital appreciation within the dividend growth portion.

Building Our Factory

It is time to start building our Income Factory, which means selecting the machines (i.e., the investments) we plan to hold in our portfolio that generate the income—the cash dividends and distributions—that we reinvest and compound to create our long-term growth. In this chapter we create a starter list of Income Factory candidate funds, from which we select the funds for our various model portfolios.

The funds in our starter list represent a range of asset classes and risk/reward profiles. If you bought the entire list, you would have a portfolio that provides a steady river of cash averaging about 9% per year. That's a rate, as we have seen, that will double and redouble itself every 8 years, so a $10,000-per-year income stream would grow to over 30 times its original amount over 40 years.

In selecting our initial Income Factory candidate funds, we assume we are investing in a tax-deferred account, like an IRA, since the overwhelming majority of individually invested retirement assets are in tax-deferred accounts. In later chapters we introduce alternative Income Factory portfolios to accommodate various investing styles and tax situations, including one for taxable accounts.

We select the candidates for our starter portfolio from among funds that invest in the basic asset classes we have already mentioned, including dividend-paying equity, utilities and infrastructure, real estate, financial and banking sectors, high-yield bonds, corporate loans, preferred stock, convertible bonds, and energy and master limited partnerships (MLPs).

For those who want to spice up their risk/reward profile a bit, in later chapters we list additional investment choices that can be added in varied proportions, depending on each investor's personal income return target and risk tolerance.

*   *   *

Income Factory 101

Up until now, we have discussed the philosophy and theory behind the Income Factory strategy and the issues investors should consider when thinking of embarking on such an approach. *Now it's time to build a factory.*

We start with a generic Income Factory, one suitable for any investor looking to build an income stream yielding and compounding its growth at a rate of about 9% annually. As noted previously, such a portfolio would double and redouble its income stream approximately every 8 years, providing an equity return consistent with the needs of most long-term investors, whether 25 years old and just starting to save for retirement, or 65 years old and looking for both current income and continued growth to support themselves to their 80s and beyond.

Of course, just because we aim for a 9% total return over the long term doesn't mean we will actually achieve that. If it turns out to be 8%, 10%, or something in that general range, we will be content. There are a lot of moving parts in any investment strategy, Income Factory included. So our goal is to assemble a portfolio of all-weather funds that churn out a steady cash flow for years to come and with minimal active monitoring and management. This is not to say there won't be occasional dividend cuts (hopefully, some increases, too) or other surprises. But our goal is to collect cash at a rate that may fluc-tuate from time to time between 8% and 10% and—with constant reinvesting and compounding—continues to grow steadily through the years.

To begin the selection process, I have assembled a list of 68 funds, divided into 11 categories by industry or asset class, which we can use as our basic approved list for creating a variety of Income Factories, depending on our risk/reward preferences and the size of our port-folio. Obviously, there are no guarantees, since investing is a highly uncertain business and anyone's *opinion* (including mine) about the best course of action or which securities or funds to buy is only that—an opinion. So do your own due diligence and especially, diversify as much as possible, so any suboptimal choices we make (aka mistakes) have minimal impact.

I personally own or have owned all of these funds in my own portfolio and often assure readers of my articles that I "eat my own cooking" in terms of following my own investment strategy. But it is hardly necessary to own the entire list to create an effective Income Factory. Regard this as a menu of core fund candidates from which you can make your own selections, do your own research, and add your own favorites.

The list is diversified, with 11 separate asset classes and additional diversification within each asset class. (See Table 6.1, next page.) If investors want to keep their total list down to under 20 or so, they can achieve considerable diversification merely by choosing just one or two funds from each category. The next chapter presents some model portfolios that do just that.

I have attempted to select timeless asset classes—loans, bonds, util-ities, gas and oil pipelines, infrastructure and other dividend-paying stocks, real estate companies, preferred stocks, and convertibles—that are staples in most investors' portfolios, both institutional and retail. Within those asset classes, I have looked for funds that are sponsored by experienced fund management companies. There are no guarantees in investing, but if you diversify in terms of individual company risk (which we do by investing through funds, not by buying the stock,

TABLE 6.1 Income Factory Asset Class Distribution

Asset Class	Number of Fund Choices	Average Distribution Yield	Range of Yields Among Funds
Loans	10	7.9%	6.5%–9%
High-Yield Bonds	10	8.5%	7.75%–10.75%
Multi-Asset	7	9.5%	7.75%–11.25%
Preferreds	4	7.5%	7.50%
Convertibles	3	9.3%	9.25%–9.5%
Real Estate	6	8.1%	7%–9.5%
Utility/Infrastructure	4	7.9%	6.4%–11%
Energy & MLPs	3	12.4%	11.75%–13.5%
Finance & Banking	2	7.9%	6.5%–9.2%
Equity-Covered Call	10	9.1%	7%–12%
General Equity	9	9.1%	7.5%–11%
Total/Average Yield	**68**	**9.0%**	

bonds, or other securities issued by specific companies), and by asset class (i.e., stocks, bonds, or other unique security type or industry), you protect yourself from the risk of nonsystemic perils befalling any specific issuer, industry, or asset type. By choosing more than one fund in each asset class, we can even diversify by portfolio manager, although that is not as important as diversification by company and asset class, especially if we stick with highly regarded fund management companies.

By diversifying this way, we ensure that our overall income stream emanates from a myriad of separate sources: companies and other entities of all types, some paying interest and principal on loans, some paying dividends, others making lease payments to their real estate landlords, or paying "tolls" to oil and gas pipeline operators. Our investment bet, with such a strategy, is that "come hell or high water" the broad slice of the economy represented in our Income Factory portfolio and representing thousands of companies and other entities will continue to muddle through and make the payments they are legally and operationally committed to. So we are throwing a wide net.

In a later chapter we discuss our downside risks somewhat more specifically and mathematically, and show how various assumptions about dividend cuts or other threats to our cash flow can affect our Income Factory output. But in general, we should recognize and expect our cash flow—our river of cash—to ebb and flow as a matter of course over our 20-, 30-, or 40-year investment horizon. That's all right, and we should be prepared for it. As we have discussed several times, our long-term goal is to earn what has historically been an equity return of 8% to 10%. But it is unlikely, regardless of how careful we are in our security selection, that we will achieve a steady 8% or 10%. Changes in interest rate levels, economic growth rates, corporate profit levels, and other macro factors affect equity returns and yield levels across all asset classes.

So there may be some periods when we can achieve 10% and higher distribution yields, at reasonable risk levels, while at other times we are happy to achieve 7% or 8% returns. The key is to relentlessly reinvest and compound, so our cash income grows over time, even if the rate of that growth may vary from one period to another. That's why picking a diversified portfolio of good funds and fund managers is so important. Some funds and asset classes may react differently than others to periodic economic and financial conditions, so we shouldn't be discouraged or too worried if individual fund dividend rates rise or fall slightly from one quarter or one year to the next. As long as we are reinvesting and compounding, the overall cash stream should rise steadily.

Whether distribution yield is 8% or 10% of our portfolio market value at any given time is less important than the fact that, either way, our river of cash is probably three or four times as great as the "trickle of cash" a typical dividend growth or total return investor is enjoying. And during a downturn or bear market our high-yielding cash income stream is a lot more comforting and makes staying the course a lot easier.

Income Factory Candidates

Here is our core list of fund candidates, broken into two lists: fixed income and equities. Given our goal of emphasizing current cash income rather than growth, even our equity choices are concentrated in sectors that pay out most of their earnings in cash dividends. In my portfolio I hold a blend of the entire risk/reward spectrum. I look to the higher-yielding funds to boost my overall return and view the lower-yielding funds as the "anchor" investments that provide long-term stability.

TABLE 6.2 Income Factory Fund Candidates (Part 1—Fixed Income)

Asset Class	Fund Name	Fund Symbol	Distribution Yield	Premium/ Discount
Senior Loans	Blackstone/GSO LS Credit	BGX	9.00%	−3.00%
	Blackstone/GSO Strategic Credit	BGB	9.00%	−7.00%
	Ares Dynamic Credit Allocation	ARDC	8.50%	−12.00%
	Apollo Floating Rate	AFT	8.00%	−12.00%
	THL Credit Senior Loan	TSLF	8.00%	−12.00%
	Nuveen Short Duration Credit Opps	JSD	8.00%	−8.00%
	Black Rock Debt Strategies	DSU	7.50%	−12.00%
	Invesco VK Dynamic Credit Opportunity	VTA	7.00%	−11.00%
	Nuveen Floating Rate Income Opportunities	JRO	7.50%	−11.00%
	Eaton Vance Senior Floating Rate	EFR	6.50%	−11.00%
	Average		**7.90%**	**−9.90%**
High Yield	Barings Global Short Duration	BGH	10.00%	−4.00%
	MFS Intermediate High Income	CIF	9.50%	−3.00%
	KKR Income Opportunities	KIO	9.50%	−4.00%
	Dreyfus High Yield Strategies	DHF	8.50%	−8.00%
	Credit Suisse Asset Management Income	CIK	8.50%	−9.00%
	Apollo Tactical Income	AIF	8.00%	−12.00%
	Black Rock Corporate High Yield	HYT	8.00%	−9.00%
	Pimco Dynamic Credit Income	PCI	8.00%	3.00%
	Barings Corporate Investors	MCI	7.75%	4.00%
	New America High Income	HYB	7.50%	−11.00%
	Average		**8.53%**	**−4.82%**

Asset Class	Fund Name	Fund Symbol	Distribution Yield	Premium/ Discount
Multi-Asset	AGIC Convertible & Income I	NCV	11.25%	0.75%
	AGIC Convertible & Income II	NCZ	10.50%	0.50%
	Brookfield Real Assets	RA	10.75%	−7.00%
	Wells Fargo Multi-Sector Income	ERC	9.50%	−5.00%
	Yield Shares High Income ETF	YYY	9.00%	NA
	Cohen & Steers Closed End Opportunity	FOF	8.00%	−3.00%
	Calamos Strategic Total Return	CSQ	7.75%	−2.00%
	Average		**9.54%**	**−2.63%**
Preferreds	First Trust Intermediate Duration Preferred & Income	FPF	7.50%	−3.00%
	Cohen & Steers Limited Duration Preferred & Income	LDP	7.50%	−2.00%
	Nuveen Preferred & Income Opportunities	JPC	7.50%	−2.00%
	JH Preferred Income III	HPS	7.50%	3.00%
	Average		**7.50%**	**−1.75%**
Convertibles	Calamos Convertible & High Income	CHY	9.25%	−3.00%
	Calamos Convertible Opportunities & Income	CHI	9.25%	−3.00%
	Advent Convertible & Income	AVK	9.50%	−10.00%
	Average		**9.33%**	**−5.33%**

At the top of our fixed-income candidates list (Table 6.2) is the *senior loan* segment. We have included 10 closed-end funds, all of which own mostly senior secured corporate loans. These are loans underwritten and syndicated by major banks (e.g., JP Morgan, Bank of America, Citibank, Goldman Sachs, Credit Suisse) to multinational corporations. The loans are secured, usually by all or most of the assets of the borrowing corporation, which means that even when they default, loan recoveries have historically been 75% of principal, which is considerably higher than the average 50% recoveries when corporate bonds (which are usually unsecured) default. Since *losses* on defaulted bonds and loans are 100% minus the average recovery rate, it means average loan losses are only about 25% versus an average loss of 50% on defaulted bonds. This results in overall portfolio credit losses for loans being only half those of high-yield bonds, which is why loans are considered so much less risky than bonds, even though the two asset classes both involve extending credit to the same cohort of companies: non-investment grade, also know as "junk."

That is a serious misnomer, since the great majority of all companies are non-investment grade, and any investor who buys stock in mid-cap or small-cap companies is actually investing in companies that are virtually 100% non-investment grade. So in putting corporate loans and high-yield bonds in our Income Factories, we are taking no more risk than typical equity investors who hold mid-caps and small-caps. Less risk actually, since loans and bonds are higher up the capital structure than equity and therefore have to be paid off in full if the equity is to have any value whatsoever.

Our loan funds represent some of the top closed-end fund managers and corporate loan specialists in the financial markets: Eaton Vance, Blackstone, Nuveen, Black Rock, Ares, Apollo, THL, Invesco. The range of distribution yields from 6% to 9% reflects that some are more conservative than others in their credit selection and in what other asset classes besides loans (like high-yield bonds) they may add to their portfolio mix. Readers are encouraged to look up the individual funds (a good reference source that many closed-end fund investors, including me, use is https://www.cefconnect.com) to get the latest data on their current pricing, yield, and premium/discount before making portfolio decisions.

In our *high-yield bond* fund segment, we have 10 funds for your consideration, again all managed by highly experienced investment firms: Barings (owned by Mass Mutual, a personal favorite in the credit space), MFS, KKR, Credit Suisse, PIMCO, T. Rowe Price, Dreyfus, and Black Rock. As mentioned already, bonds are a bit riskier than loans because they are further down the balance sheet and therefore behind loans in line for payment if the issuer defaults. That's why we see a higher range of distribution yields in our high-yield bond fund candidate list (7.5% up to 10%, or an average yield of 8.5%) compared to a slightly lower range of yields (6% to 9%, averaging just below 8%) in the loan space.

As we noted in discussing loans, the terms *high yield* and *junk* scare a lot of investors, but the high-yield loan and bond sectors have a good record for coming through economic and financial cycles intact, if you are a long-term, diversified investor. Individual companies can go off the rails, and do, all the time, so personally I would never buy specific loans or bonds because you can't ever know when lightning might strike a particular company. But diversified portfolios—that is, funds—of loans and bonds have done well through all sorts of cycles, including the "great recession" in 2008. Market prices hit the skids and healthy performing loans and bonds were selling for 60 cents on the dollar or even less, but the asset class came through undamaged and investors who stayed the course, or better yet, reinvested at the bargain prices Mr. Market made available, did very well.

The range in bond fund yields, just like with the loan funds, reflects each fund's approach to both credit selection and the degree it chooses to be somewhat adventurous in assembling its own portfolio. Barings Global Short Duration (BGH), one of our highest yielding high-yield funds, is actually a hybrid, with a wide assortment of secured and unsecured loans and bonds, and other fixed-income securities. Similarly KKR Income Opportunities (KIO), Apollo Tactical Income (AIF), and PIMCO Dynamic Credit Income (PCI) have broad mandates that encompass the entire high-yield spectrum. The other funds on our list focus somewhat more on traditional high-yield bonds, although not necessarily exclusively. I think it is to our benefit if our funds' portfolio managers have the freedom to be opportunistic in and around their respective target markets. That allows them to take advantage of market pricing anomalies, which can become substantial in less liquid markets (like high-yield bonds and loans) during periods of market turbulence. Barings Corporate Investors (MCI) and New America High Income (HYB) are at the lower end of this category's yield spectrum. But they are two of the most solid, reputable "buy 'em and forget 'em" funds in the business, with excellent long-term records that go back over 40 years and 30 years, respectively.

Our *multi-asset* segment includes seven funds, six of them closed-end funds and one exchange-traded fund (ETF). The highest yielders are the two AGIC Convertible & Income Funds, numbers 1 and 2, and Brookfield Real Assets (RA). The AGIC funds have a flexible mandate and hold an assortment of higher-yielding assets, including debt, convertibles, and preferreds. Brookfield (RA) holds a variety of loans, bonds, and stock, all of which involve ownership or claims against what it regards as *real* assets, defined as "real estate, infrastructure and natural resources." Brookfield is part of the Brookfield Asset Management group, which is over 100 years old, based in Toronto, and one of the most successful and respected asset managers in the world. That doesn't mean RA won't have its ups and downs over the years, but like all of the investments we select, we believe it is in a good position to weather any short-term challenges. Two of our funds—Wells Fargo Multi-Sector Income (ERC) and Calamos Strategic Total Return (CSQ)—are broad mission, go-anywhere funds with solid managers and good long-term records.

Our other two multi-asset funds are actually "funds of funds," each owning broad portfolios of closed-end funds. This provides maximum diversification across individual companies, asset classes, and fund managers. Cohen & Steers Closed End Opportunity (FOF) has been a favorite of mine for years, providing a steady distribution of 8% or more and professionally managed exposure to the entire closed-end fund market. Yield Shares High Income ETF (YYY) is an ETF linked to the ISE High Income™ closed-end fund index that tracks what it considers to be the 30 most attractively priced and liquid closed-end funds. YYY and FOF tend to perform somewhat similarly over time.

The *preferreds* category is one of our "engine room" asset classes, boring and unexciting but cranking out dependable cash flows month after month. Our four preferred stock funds are managed by highly respected fund families—John Hancock, First Trust, Cohen & Steers, and Nuveen. Nothing exciting, just steady income in the 7% to 8% range. While this is at the low end of our target yield range, the stability of this asset category helps offset some of the riskier securities at the other end of our risk/reward scale. Preferred stocks, as many readers know, behave more like bonds than stocks. As a form of equity, they are lower down the totem pole than loans or bonds, and therefore generally have to pay higher yields than bonds of a similar credit quality, which in this case is predominantly investment grade or very close to it. That means they represent a higher credit quality and lower default rate than the loans and high-yield bonds in the asset classes discussed earlier. To get close to an 8% yield for taking investment grade credit risk is a good deal for a long-term income investor.

Our final fixed-income category is *convertible bonds*. Whereas preferred *stock* actually behaves and is priced to yield more like *bonds*, convertible bonds are more the reverse. They behave more like stock, in that while they are bonds in the sense they have interest and principal that must be repaid by the issuing company, they contain an option to be converted into the issuer's stock. That gives them more upside potential than either ordinary bonds or preferred stock. (Except for "convertible preferred," which is sort of a hybrid.) The convertibles have higher yields than the preferreds (averaging over 9% versus below 8% for the preferreds), reflecting the fact that the issuers of convertibles tend to be less well-established companies rated below-investment grade, whereas the issuers of preferreds, as we just saw, are predominantly investment grade.

Our approved list of convertibles includes two Calamos funds (CHY and CHI) that I have held with good results for many years, and Advent Convertible & Income (AVK), which is a Guggenheim-sponsored fund with a good long-term record.

In summary, the fixed-income selections for our basic Income Factory include 34 funds, with distribution yields reflecting different risk/reward profiles that range from 10% to 11% at the high end of the multi-asset category to about 7% at the more conservative end of the senior loan category. So there is considerable latitude for investors to mix and match to create a portfolio as large (i.e., all 34 funds) or as streamlined (perhaps 10 to 12 funds) as they wish, and with a variety of risk/reward profiles. As we turn now to our equity fund selections, we see that we have a similar range of choices.

TABLE 6.3 Income Factory Fund Candidates (Part 2—Equities)

Asset Class	Fund Name	Fund Symbol	Distribution Yield	Premium/ Discount
Real Estate	Aberdeen Global Premier Properties	AWP	9.50%	−8.00%
	Neuberger Berman Real Estate	NRO	9.50%	−7.50%
	CBRE Clarion Global Real Estate	IGR	8.00%	−13.00%
	Nuveen Real Asset Income & Growth	JRI	7.60%	−12.00%
	Cohen & Steers Quality Income Realty	RQI	7.00%	−2.00%
	Nuveen Real Estate Income	JRS	7.25%	−5.00%
	Average		**8.14%**	**−6.79%**
Utility/ Infrastructure	Macquarie/First Trust Global Infrastructure	MFD	11.00%	−2.00%
	Cohen & Steers Infrastructure	UTF	7.25%	−5.00%
	Macquarie Global Infrastructure	MGU	7.00%	−13.00%
	Gabelli Global Utility & Income	GLU	6.40%	−6.00%
	Average		**7.91%**	**−6.50%**
Energy & MLPs	Fiduciary Claymore Energy Infrastructure	FMO	13.50%	−7.00%
	Nuveen All Cap Energy MLP Opportunity	JMLP	12.00%	−10.00%
	Tortoise Energy Infrastructure	TYG	11.75%	−3.00%
	Average		**12.42%**	**−6.67%**
Finance	First Trust Specialty Finance	FGB	9.20%	0.00%
	John Hancock Financial Opportunities	BTO	6.5%	−2.00%
	Average		**7.90%**	**−1.00%**
Equity - Covered Call	Guggenheim Enhanced Equity Income	GPM	12.00%	1.00%
	Voya Global Equity Dividend & Premium Opportunity	IGD	11.50%	−7.00%
	Eaton Vance Tax-Managed Buy-Write Opportunity	ETV	9.00%	5.00%
	Cohen & Steers Global Income Builder	INB	8.50%	−7.00%
	Eaton Vance Tax-Managed Global	EXG	9.00%	−6.00%
	Eaton Vance Tax-Managed Dividend Equity	ETY	8.50%	0.00%
	Eaton Vance Tax-Managed Global Buy-Write	ETW	9.00%	−5.00%
	Voya Global Advantage & Opportunity	IGA	8.75%	−8.00%
	First Trust Enhanced Equity	FFA	7.50%	−4.00%
	Nuveen Nasdaq 100 Dynamic Overwrite	QQQX	7.00%	−2.00%
	Average		**9.08%**	**−3.30%**

Asset Class	Fund Name	Fund Symbol	Distribution Yield	Premium/ Discount
General Equity	Guggenheim Strategic Opportunity	GOF	10.75%	15.00%
	Liberty All-Star Equity	USA	10.75%	−4.00%
	Gabelli Equity	GAB	9.75%	6.00%
	Gabelli Convertible & Income	GCV	9.40%	−4.00%
	Eaton Vance Tax Advantaged Global Dividend	ETO	9.00%	2.50%
	Nuveen Tax Advantaged Total Return	JTA	8.50%	−5.00%
	Calamos Strategic Total Return	CSQ	7.75%	−2.00%
	Nuveen Tax Advantaged Dividend Growth	JTD	7.50%	−3.00%
	Royce Value	RVT	8.25%	−11.00%
Average			**9.07%**	**−2.28%**

Because our Income Factory emphasizes current cash dividends over longer-term growth, it is no surprise that even our equity fund portfolio (Table 6.3) is heavily weighted toward traditional income stocks. But a common theme running through our equity fund selections is that while they have to offer us substantial cash dividend yields, we won't complain if some of them also provide modest market appreciation on top of their cash returns. We have said repeatedly that an Income Factory's purpose is to create its own growth by reinvesting and compounding cash distributions. But we won't look a gift horse in the mouth if some of the rivers of cash our Factory produces also provide a little market growth while pumping out that cash.

An important example of that is our *real estate* portfolio, which contains seven high-quality funds from top fund families, several of which we have already encountered in other asset categories: Cohen & Steers, Nuveen, Neuberger Berman, Aberdeen, and CBRE Clarion. Our real estate funds distribute yields ranging from 7% to over 9%, reflecting the greater range of credit risk and global reach of several of the funds. We welcome the variety of risk/reward profiles represented by these seven funds, as long as we have the diversification to offset it.

By its nature, real estate investing is particularly suited to our Income Factory philosophy. Typical long-term real estate investors purchase a property for its income potential, harvesting the steady cash—and therefore the property's economic value—from lease payments over many years. They don't spend much time worrying about its resale value during the 20- or 30-year lease period. But our typical real estate investor is not opposed to getting some growth along with their income stream. Nor are we in our Income Factory, and a number of our real estate funds (specifically the two Cohen & Steers funds and the Neuberger Berman) have provided considerable market appreciation in addition to their generous yields over the past 10 years.

Utility/infrastructure funds are also logical candidates for an Income Factory. The entities they hold provide essential economic services and once fully established, often have what analysts call "deep moats" around them, given the complete or partial monopoly many of them have in their core businesses. As a result they are deliberately structured financially to generate steady income to service their debt and attract long-term capital. To use the horse race analogy introduced earlier, utilities and infrastructure projects are designed to finish the race (in fact, a very long race) by staying in business, repaying their debt, and building value over the long term.

Our utility fund choices, like our real estate funds, follow the general rule of our other Income Factory investments that market appreciation—if any—is the icing on the cake, with cash distributions being the cake itself. Cohen & Steers Infrastructure (UTF) focuses mostly on utilities, although with a broader international mandate, and has performed well in terms of both appreciation and cash income over the past decade. Gabelli Global Utility & Income (GLU) has a solid long-term record as does the Gabelli family of funds in general. The two Macquarie funds (MFD and MGU) are both consistent long-term performers with broad mandates to seek both income and total return in the global infrastructure arena.

One of my favorite closed-end funds, Reaves Utility Income (UTG), is a victim of its own success, having appreciated to a point where its current yield recently fell to just below 6% and its market price crossed into premium territory. So while I have held it for many years and commend it to readers as a great buy-and-hold-forever fund, its yield is currently too low to meet our Income Factory criteria for new purchases. But if it slumps and its dividend yield creeps up to 6.5% or higher, then it becomes—once again—a serious Income Factory candidate.

Our *energy & MLP* sector is a more focused and specialized subsector of the broader utility and infrastructure universe. MLPs are limited by law to investments in real estate and energy, with energy infrastructure (i.e., pipelines, storage, and transportation) accounting for over 80% of all MLPs. Besides having the primary advantage mentioned earlier for other utilities and infrastructure—steady income from essential "deep moat" businesses—MLPs also have a tax advantage of being pass-through vehicles that don't pay tax before making distributions to their shareholders. This boosts their cash flow to the shareholders from what it would be if they were organized in a more traditional corporate form. The one disadvantage with MLPs is that there are potential tax complications when they are held in tax-deferred vehicles like IRAs. Fortunately, that problem is eliminated if the IRA holds closed-end funds that hold the MLPs rather than holding them directly.

There are lots of good MLP funds, and we have selected three with experienced management and good records: Fiduciary Claymore Energy Infrastructure (FMO), Nuveen All Cap Energy MLP Opportunity (JMLP), and Tortoise Energy Infrastructure (TYN). The MLP sector has been selling at historical lows in recent years, which has driven distribution yields to very high levels, even though many analysts see no permanent threats to the sector's longer-term viability. Currently yielding in the 11% to 13% range, the MLP fund sector contains some of our Income Factory's highest-yielding funds.

Our *finance* industry funds are very different from one another, yet each is equally attractive in its own way. First Trust Specialty Finance (FGB) has been one of my personal favorite funds for years and is also among the largest holdings in my own original Income Factory. It primarily invests in the stock of business development companies (BDCs), which are specialized lenders to small and medium-sized businesses. That's about 90% of FGB's portfolio, with mortgage real estate investment trusts (mREITs) making up the other 10%. FGB had paid a steady or rising distribution for the past 10 years, with its yield varying within the 9% to 11% range, although the fund recently announced a dividend reduction from 11% to 9%. Timing our pur- chases to coincide with lower price points and higher distribution yields is ideal, but not always possible. Even when I have purchased FGB at its higher price/lower yield points, it has been a solid portfolio performer and cash income generator.

Unlike FGB's focus on small business lenders, John Hancock Finan- cial Opportunities fund (BTO) owns a highly diversified portfolio of some of the largest and most successful banks in the country. With the two funds together, our finance industry portfolio provides sort of a "barbell" strategy, representing both ends of the big lender/small lender spectrum. It delivers a blended distribution yield of almost 8%, along with demonstrated growth potential (from BTO, not from FGB whose generous yield in the 9% range meets our long-term goal, even if it never increases).

BTO has been a great performer, even though its 6.5% yield is at the lower end of the range we normally consider for our Income Fac- tory. But it ranks up there with previously described Reeves Utility Income (UTG) as one of those superstar long-term holds that has demonstrated its ability to pay a generous yield and grow at the same time. Its current yield of 6.5% is still attractive for a fund that offers a history of steady growth along with it. If I were to wander at all from my normal high-yield/no (or minimal) growth strategy, these two funds—BTO and UTG—would be good ones to do it with.

Our *equity-covered call* portfolio is uniquely suited to a long-term Income Factory strategy. These are closed-end funds that hold tra- ditional equity, but enhance their cash dividend by selling calls (i.e., options) on the stock. The premiums from the calls boost the funds' cash flows, but the calls themselves trade away some of the potential appreciation if their portfolios increase in market value. Of course, the additional cash flow also cushions the short-term pain if the stocks drop in value. Either way it is available to boost the dividend above what it would otherwise be if there were no premiums.

Obviously, there are no free lunches in investing or anything else. Covered call strategies are ideal for investors who value steady cash distributions more than they do capital appreciation and are willing to trade off the latter for the former. By holding them in closed-end funds we get the additional opportunity to buy at a discount if we time our entry appropriately, which means we have more assets working for us than we actually paid for, providing an extra boost to current income.

Our 10 equity-covered call fund choices provide us with a good selection of all-weather performers in this asset class, from many of the top fund families we have encountered before. Since fund managers, even within the same asset class, typically have their own unique portfolio strategy, I recommend "manager diversification" as well as portfolio diversification. This list allows investors to choose among four funds from Eaton Vance, which has broad experience in the covered-call category, two from Voya, and one each from Guggenheim, Cohen & Steers, Nuveen, and First Trust.

Our final category is *general equity*, where again we present a range of choices to suit various styles and representing well-respected fund families, including Gabelli, Eaton Vance, Nuveen, Calamos, Guggenheim, ALPS, and Royce. Unlike our fixed-income asset classes and our quasi-fixed-income equities, like real estate, utility/infrastructure, and energy and MLPs that produce "generic" income sufficient enough to cover their generous distributions, more traditional equity portfolios do not normally, from their own portfolio cash flow, produce dividends sufficient to support 7% to 10% payments to fund shareholders. That means they have to supplement their income stream from additional sources. We saw how equity-covered call funds do this by selling off options on some or all of their portfolio's potential appreciation.

The general equity funds cover their potential cash flow shortfall primarily in two ways: leverage and capital gains. Leverage is fairly straightforward and predictable. As institutional investors and money managers, typical closed-end funds have access to loan facilities at very attractive interest rates, so they can leverage themselves in an amount up to 50% of their equity at rates that often are in the low single digits (2% to 3%). They can use the loan proceeds, of course, to buy whatever their fund's target asset class is, earning a much higher rate of return on the newly acquired assets than they are paying on their borrowed leverage. This can add an additional 2% (or more) to the fund's net shareholder return (i.e., after the cost of the leverage).

Besides its use by equity funds, leverage is particularly advantageous for funds that invest in higher-yielding asset classes, where the gap between the leverage cost and the yield on fund assets is especially wide. For example, 2% to 3% leverage cost versus 6% to 8% yields in a senior loan or high-yield bond fund could result in an additional 4% to 6% spread on the portion of the portfolio leveraged.

Virtually all of our general equity funds use leverage to boost their returns (the Liberty All-Star fund being an exception). In addition to leverage, the funds typically use capital gains to help maintain their distributions. This means they have to be nimble traders and/or stock pickers to be sure they are returning real income to shareholders and not just returning their own capital to them. Getting some of our own capital back as a distribution is less of a problem if we are constantly reinvesting our dividends. But we need to monitor the source of our distributions if we want to understand what our actual return is.

As we have said previously, our Income Factory's main goal is to generate cash income with little emphasis on growth, other than the growth we create through our own reinvesting and compounding. But investors that do want to emphasize growth a bit more should look for it in the equity categories. The funds in our general equity category all have a history of producing occasional growth over and above their distributions, so a diversified assortment of them, along with other funds like UTG and BTO, could provide that element of additional growth some investors are looking for.

Next Steps: Assembling the Factory

Now we have a core list of 68 funds from which to assemble our Income Factory. Obviously, one could buy all 68, which I have done, in one portfolio or another, but 68 funds may be more than many investors want or need, depending on the size of their portfolios or the amount of diversification they are looking for. A portfolio that held equal positions in each of the 68 funds would generate a distribution yield of about 9%, based on recent prices and yields, but that figure will fluctuate over time as market prices change.

I suggest thinking of this as an approved list from which to select funds for our own personal portfolios. Although these are all quality funds managed by respected fund managers, not all of them will be equally appealing at their current prices and yields at any particular time. Therefore, investors may wish to review the list prior to purchasing funds for their own Income Factories to see which ones are most attractively priced in terms of distribution yield and discount. In our next chapter we construct a number of model portfolios based on selections from this list, and later suggest various other funds that can be used to spice them up in terms of increasing their risk/reward profiles, for investors so inclined.

Income Factory Model Portfolios

If the list of 68 fund candidates for our Income Factory introduced in the last chapter seems a little overwhelming, you need not worry. In this chapter we pare that list down into bite-sized model portfolios designed to suit individual investors' risk/reward preferences as well as their portfolio sizes.

Our four basic model portfolios consist of:

- An aggressive risk/reward portfolio of 12 funds targeting the higher-yielding end of each of the asset classes in our candidate list of 68 funds, but still intended to be a low-maintenance portfolio. If held in equal amounts, the 12 funds should generate a distribution yield above 10%
- An aggressive risk/reward portfolio of 20 funds, still targeting the higher-yielding end of the asset classes in our target list, but with a greater number of funds to allow sufficient diversification for investors with larger portfolios
- A moderate risk/reward portfolio of 12 funds for investors who want modest risk and low maintenance, diversified among a dozen

funds mostly in separate asset classes. Solid "one decision" funds
that generate an average distribution yield above 8%
■ A moderate risk/reward portfolio of 24 funds for the same investor
who has a larger portfolio and desires more diversification

There is no guarantee the more aggressive risk/reward portfolios will
generate higher returns and a larger ultimate income stream over the long
term. We expect they probably will, but they may also generate somewhat
more excitement and potential angst along the way since higher yields
carry greater risk of occasional cuts. Our moderate risk/reward portfolios
promise a somewhat lower yield to begin with, so they are less likely to
disappoint, providing a more stress-free ride for investors.

*   *   *

In the last chapter we introduced "Income Factory 101," a generic list
of 68 all-weather funds from respected fund families, representing 11
asset classes. These are all funds that I hold myself, either in a personal
portfolio or one I manage for close friends and family. Moreover I
believe they comprise—as a diversified group—the sort of portfolio
any of us could hold indefinitely with minimal monitoring and know
that our income stream would continue to accumulate in a reasonably
predictable manner.

In other words, a portfolio that would behave as an Income Factory is supposed to, generating steady dividends and distributions that
can be reinvested and compounded to produce a constantly growing
"factory output" of cash. This is not to suggest that the market value
may not fluctuate over time or that it might not drop or otherwise fail
to grow over long periods of time. Every investor embarking on an
Income Factory strategy has to remind himself or herself that this is all
about growing long-term income, and that market price appreciation,
while nice if we get it, is not an essential part of the program. This
shouldn't be a surprise to any reader, by now, but it is worth emphasizing again at this point where we are introducing actual investments
and portfolios.

Risk/Reward and Other Choices

Very few readers want to start out with all 68 funds. First of all, it isn't practical unless you have a portfolio that justifies that many separate funds. Even for someone with a $2 million portfolio, 68 funds would work out to an average exposure of about $30,000 per fund, probably more diversification than they need.

So I suggest we think of this as an "approved list" from which investors can make their own choices and assemble their own port-folios. Many readers will choose to do their own research, prune the list, add to it, or both. In addition, we will update the data in this list periodically, with current distribution yield and premium/discount information. Links to the online updates are included in Chapter 1.

But to help make it simple for many investors to get started, we have created model portfolios of different sizes and varying risk/reward profiles, so investors will have choices they can match up with their own personal needs and investing inclinations.

For example, someone with a $100,000 to $200,000 portfo-lio might feel that 20 funds and an average hold size of $5,000 to $10,000 would be appropriate. Other investors may want to keep things simpler and limit their portfolio to only 10 or 12 funds, or even fewer. Since these are diversified funds, and not the stocks or bonds of individual companies, there is obviously far less concentration risk in holding 10 or 12 funds than there would be in holding that same number or even many times that number of discrete companies. Inves-tors with more sizable portfolios can choose one of the larger models if they wish to spread their investments among a greater number of funds.

Aggressive Risk/Reward Profile—12 Funds

Our first model portfolio targets the aggressive risk/reward end of the spectrum, but keeps the size of the portfolio manageable with only 12 funds (Table 7.1). In most cases we have selected the highest-yielding fund in each category, although in the equity-covered call category we included the highest-yielding fund—Guggenheim Enhanced Equity

Income (GPM)—along with solid performer Voya Global Advantage & Premium Opportunity (IGA) to round it up to an even dozen.

TABLE 7.1 Income Factory Model Portfolio
(Aggressive Risk/Reward—12 Funds)

Asset Class	Fund Name	Fund Symbol	Distribution Yield	Premium/ Discount
Senior Loans	Blackstone/GSO Strategic Credit	BGB	9.0%	–7.0%
High Yield	Barings Global Short Duration	BGH	10.0%	–4.0%
Multi-Asset	Brookfield Real Assets	RA	10.8%	–7.0%
Preferreds	Cohen & Steers Ltd Duration Preferred & income	LDP	7.5%	–2.0%
Convertibles	Calamos Convertible & High Income	CHY	9.3%	–3.0%
Real Estate	Aberdeen Global Premier Properties	AWP	9.5%	–8.0%
Utility/ Infrastructure	Macquarie/First Trust Global Infrastructure	MFD	11.0%	–2.0%
Energy & MLPs	Fiduciary Claymore Energy Infrastructure	FMO	13.5%	–7.0%
Finance	First Trust Specialty Finance	FGB	9.2%	0.0%
Equity - Covered Call	Guggenheim Enhanced Equity Income	GPM	12.0%	1.0%
	Voya Global Advantage & Premium Opportunity	IGA	8.8%	–6.0%
General Equity	Liberty All-Star Equity	USA	10.8%	–4.0%
Average			10.1%	–4.1%

With only 12 funds to monitor and manage, this is a fairly low-maintenance portfolio. But it contains all of our major targeted asset classes, each represented by one or more solid funds from reputable fund managers. The distribution yield, if an investor holds an equal amount of each fund, is slightly above 10%. If reinvested and compounded at that rate, an investor's original income stream would double and redouble about every seven years. Of course, there are no guarantees. Suppose, for example, the average yield fell, because of distribution cuts, to—let us say—9%. Then the rate of doubling and redoubling would slow down to every eight years, which is still a very healthy growth rate.

This will be a familiar pattern as we model various portfolios of funds that hold high-yield asset classes. Because of the wide diversi-fication within the different funds, when a fund cuts its dividend, it is generally because of dividend cuts among a subset of that fund's own portfolio, not across the board for all the fund's holdings. This obviously affects the fund's dividend, but in most cases does not sub-stantially reduce it or eliminate it. This is how the risk of dividend cuts in funds differs from that of individual companies. When spe-cific companies have cash flow problems and have to cut dividends, it is often serious enough that the entire dividend or a substantial por-tion of it is cut. But when we model broadly diversified portfolios, it is reasonable to project partial dividend reductions, not the sort of dra-conian cuts that befall individual companies.

Investors who want to increase the risk/reward profile of the model are free to vary the proportions of each asset class, skewing it more toward the equity side and lightening up on, say, senior loans or pre-ferreds. For example, they might wish to boost the holding of First Trust Specialty Finance (FGB), a fund with a widely diversified port-folio of small business lenders and investors, and reduce Blackstone/ GSO Strategic Credit (BGX), since both asset classes reflect a some-what similar bet on the macro-economy. FGB represents equity in companies that lend to small and mid-size companies, while senior loan funds like BGX invest in loans to large, multinational compa-nies. But they are both essentially bets on the overall economy and assume that when large companies (as a group) do well and meet their loan commitments, smaller companies (again, as a group) also do well. Small and mid-size companies tend to have lower credit ratings than large multinationals, and therefore pay higher interest rates, which explains why FGB's investments pay higher dividends and allow FGB (typically but not always) to pass on higher distributions to its share-holders than those paid by BGB and other senior loan funds.

Aggressive Risk/Reward Profile—20 Funds

Our next model portfolio (Table 7.2) targets investors who have the same aggressive risk/reward profile but want a larger list of fund candidates to choose from. We have expanded the list to 20 funds from 12, adding additional funds to our senior loan, high yield, multi-asset, convertibles, real estate, energy and MLP, and general equity categories.

TABLE 7.2 Income Factory Model Portfolio
(Aggressive Risk/Reward—20 Funds)

Asset Class	Fund Name	Fund Symbol	Distribution Yield	Premium/ Discount
Senior Loans	Blackstone/GSO Strategic Credit	BGB	9.0%	−7.0%
	Ares Dynamic Credit Allocation	ARDC	8.5%	−12.0%
High Yield	MFS Intermediate High Income	CIF	9.5%	−3.0%
	Barings Global Short Duration	BGH	10.0%	−4.0%
	KKR Income Opportunities	KIO	9.5%	−4.0%
Multi-Asset	AGIC Convertible & Income I	NCV	11.3%	0.8%
	Brookfield Real Assets	RA	10.8%	−7.0%
Preferreds	Cohen & Steers Ltd Duration Preferred & Income	LDP	7.5%	−2.0%
Convertibles	Calamos Convertible & High Income	CHY	9.3%	−3.0%
	Advent Claymore Convertible & Income	AVK	9.50%	−10.0%
Real Estate	Aberdeen Global Premier Properties	AWP	9.5%	−8.0%
	Neuberger Berman Real Estate	NRO	9.5%	−7.5%
Utility/ Infrastructure	Macquarie/First Trust Global Infrastructure	MFD	10.8%	−2.0%
Energy & MLPs	Fiduciary Claymore Energy Infrastructure	FMO	13.5%	−7.0%
	Nuveen All Cap Energy MLP Opportunity	JMLP	12.0%	−10.0%
Finance	First Trust Specialty Finance	FGB	9.2%	0.0%

Asset Class	Fund Name	Fund Symbol	Distribution Yield	Premium/ Discount
Equity- Covered Call	Guggenheim Enhanced Equity Income	GPM	12.0%	1.0%
	Voya Global Advantage & Premium Opportunity	IGA	8.8%	−6.0%
General Equity	Liberty All-Star Equity	USA	10.8%	−4.0%
	Guggenheim Strategic Opportunity Fund	GOF	10.8%	15.0%
Average			10.1%	−4.0%

The 8 new funds pay slightly lower yields than the original 12, but the impact on the overall distribution yield is negligible. Most investors would probably regard that as a reasonable price to pay for the additional diversification.

"Aggressive"—What's in a Name?
(a Digression on Aggression)
This is a good point at which to discuss "aggressive" and how we define it. We have said that a long-term equity return has historically been in the range of 8% to 10%. Even a 7% or 8% return, reinvested, compounded, and sustained over 30 or 40 years is better than most investors achieve if they move in and out of the market at various times trying to avoid downturns or take advantage of anticipated upturns. So the model portfolios we create in this chapter and the next target the following ranges:

- Close to 10% for those labeled "aggressive," with all of it earned in the form of distribution yield
- In the 8% to 8.5% range if described as "moderate," again with all of it earned as cash distribution
- The same ranges apply to those models we designate as Income Factory Light (IFL), with outcomes dependent on (1) whether we opt for the moderate or aggressive model for the Income Factory portion, and (2) the mix of Income Factory target funds and Dividend Growth stocks we select

Labeling a strategy or portfolio "aggressive" does not necessarily ensure that it will achieve higher returns over the long term, given that higher yields sometimes turn out to be less sustainable than more modest ones. Since our Income Factory strategy is to emphasize current cash income as our primary source of growth, the term *aggressive* from our perspective means emphasizing and maximizing our distribution yield. In other words, it means pushing to our own risk tolerance limits the amount of distribution yield we aim for in our portfolio.

Conventional wisdom would suggest that, other things being equal, by pushing the envelope on yield, we should end up with a riskier portfolio, including the whole range of risks we discussed earlier, like:

- Risk of market price decline and/or volatility
- Risk of a distribution cut if the underlying assets held by the funds fail to make the payments needed to support the fund's distribution level
- Liquidity risk of being unable to sell out at a reasonable price when we want to
- Complexity risk (requiring extra due diligence and analysis to understand the asset class)

These are the risks we live with in the high-yield world, and the risks get greater as we move further out the yield spectrum. But fortunately, as we discussed earlier, some of these risks help drive the market price down and the yield we receive up, while representing risks that we, as long-term investors, do not actually need to be too worried about. In fact, the only risk I think is all that relevant to long-term Income Factory investors is the potential risk of distribution cuts, and even those risks can be mitigated somewhat through diversification and by managing our own expectations.

Distribution cuts generally occur because of credit defaults or dividend cuts by the underlying corporate entities in the portfolio, or by macroeconomic events that cause interest rates to shift in a way that affects the return expectations for our fund or asset class. This happened to a lot of asset classes about 10 years ago when the Fed reduced interest rates to such a low point that returns dropped across the board, and PIMCO executives at the time Mohamed El-Erian and Bill Gross coined the term *new normal* to suggest that investor expectations about a satisfactory long-term return had shifted downward. It would certainly cause our projected distribution levels to drop if bonds, loans, or other fixed-income assets we held had to be replaced with lower-yielding assets when they matured, and those lower-yield expectations would eventually filter through the financial markets generally.

Increases in interest rates can also affect a fund's ability to make distribution payments. Typically, rising interest rates increase the leverage costs for a fund, so the interest the fund pays to borrow the funds it uses to buy additional earning assets may increase immediately, but there may be a lag before the earnings on the fund's assets rise to match the added leverage cost. That shrinks the net profit margin, or "spread," on the fund's portfolio, constricting the available cash flow that supports the distributions.

Whether the fund's net margin shrinks because its underlying assets fail to perform due to defaults or dividend cuts, or because of macroeconomic changes to interest rates or earnings levels, the result is the same: our distribution may be cut. The cut might be temporary, for a short period of time while the fund's earning assets reprice themselves upward if they are floating rate, or mature and are replaced with higher-yielding assets if they are fixed rate. Or it might be a more permanent cut.

I tend to be philosophical about distribution cuts. Knowing that events like this happen to even the best managed funds, we can adopt several mind-sets. We can choose to essentially "live with" the risk and deliberately buy many funds that we know may have to cut their distributions at some point, but take the attitude that we enjoy the higher distributions while we can and deal with the consequences when and if the distribution cut takes place later on. Alternatively, we can take the attitude that we wish to avoid distribution cuts at all costs (well, *almost* all costs, since lightning can strike anywhere), and deliberately buy funds with more modest, sustainable dividends to begin with.

My personal approach has been to spice up my portfolio with a number of funds that pay higher than normal distributions, knowing full well that a few of them will end up reducing their payments at some point in the future. I figure that if I capture and reinvest the higher distribution for some period of time and then the fund reduces it later on to what turns out to be a more sustainable level, then I am ahead of the game because at least I got a "windfall" yield for a while. I figure that I am certainly no worse off than where I would have been if I had settled for funds that paid only "normal" distributions and limited my investments to them right from the start.

"But hold on a minute," some readers may be saying. "What about the drop in market price that the distribution cut has likely precipitated?" That is a valid question. There are two answers, each one only partially satisfying, but together I find them close enough to being reassuring that I haven't changed my strategy. First of all, if I am in it for the long haul, the drop in price as a result of a decrease in distribution will likely end up being a rounding error over the long term, as I continually reinvest and compound the cash dividends I am receiving. In fact, the distribution cut may even turn out to be temporary, since funds sometimes move their distributions up as well as down in response to changes in their underlying cash flow.

Moreover, I often find that markets can be fairly forgiving, pricewise, when a fund adjusts its distribution downward. The market seems to prefer to see a fund set its distribution yield at a level it considers sustainable than to see it stretch to pay a higher yield that it cannot really afford on a continuing basis. So often there is an immediate spike down when a fund announces a dividend cut, followed by a slow rise back up to a price level where the market deems the new distribution to be sustainable, and the yield at that price to be attractive. If you are a long-term investor, you don't care about the spike down, except as an opportunity to buy more. You are more interested in the gap between where it was originally and the new price it settles back up to once the market digests the cut. The gap between the two, which frequently is far less than the original drop, is what has to be offset by accumulated future cash distributions. As I said, it typically is not that much compared to the prospective future long-term cash stream.

In summary, the main difference I see between an aggressive approach to maximizing distributions and a more moderate one may be psychological and emotional as much as financial. Let us imagine two Income Factories, one of which strives for higher yields (10% and higher), knowing there is a good chance that the funds paying them may have to reduce their payouts at some point in the future (or alternatively, that the fund will have to dip into its capital—i.e., pay the investor some of his or her own principal—to sustain its distribution payment). The other Income Factory sets a lower long-term target for itself, and decides to invest in funds that pay distributions in the 8% range, but with more confidence that the funds selected will be able to sustain their dividends in that range indefinitely.

Which Income Factory will do better in the long term? Frankly, I don't know and we probably won't know for another decade or two. The moderate factory, like the tortoise in Aesop's famous race, may be the slow and steady one whose funds seldom miss a beat, paying their 8% like clockwork and occasionally increasing it, so after 30 years perhaps the accumulated gain will be closer to 8.5% or even 9%.

The more aggressive Income Factory may have started out shooting for 10% or 11% yields, but perhaps saw some slippage in the form of dividend cuts along the way. I would guess at that yield level there would probably be more dividend cuts than the occasional dividend increase. There was probably also some principal "erosion" as a result of the higher distribution payments including some return of capital, in addition to the actual dividend, which is often the case as you get into higher and higher yield territory. But with regular reinvestment and compounding, the factory undoubtedly grew over many years and perhaps ended up with an accumulated gain somewhere below the 10% to 11% target but still, let us hope, in the 9.5% to 10% range.

If that is how it works out, I believe both investors will be happy. The more aggressive investor achieved a higher return, and as we have seen, an extra 0.5% or 1% can make a big difference in income and wealth accumulation over many decades. At the same time, the more aggressive factory owner probably will have paid a higher price for the difference, in the form of market angst and having to work somewhat harder to follow and monitor their higher-yielding and probably more complex asset class selections.

Meanwhile the less aggressive Income Factory owner still achieved a steady, long-term compoundable cash income of over 8%, and enjoyed a smoother ride with less work and stress than the more aggressive Factory owner. As long as they made a conscious choice upfront and set their expectations realistically, they both should be happy.

In the interest of full disclosure, I should acknowledge that in my own portfolio I have attempted to achieve even higher yields than the aggressive models that we have introduced here, by using some closed-end funds that hold highly complex assets like collateralized loan obligations (CLOs) and leveraged exchange-traded notes that are linked to other financial instruments. These involve a degree of risk and complexity, with my portfolio yield target in the 11% to 12% range, that is more aggressive than what we assume here for our typical aggressive investor. In a later chapter we discuss some of these strategies in greater detail for those readers interested in a somewhat more risky and high-powered Income Factory.

Moderate Risk/Reward Profile—12 Funds

But first, let us review our moderate risk/reward 12-fund Income Factory, in Table 7.3. Designed for the investor who wants a low-maintenance portfolio with limited risk, this portfolio has a number of very solid "one decision" funds and an average distribution yield in the 8% to 8.5% range. For readers who may be familiar with our series of Income Factory articles on the Seeking Alpha website, this portfolio has many of the same risk/reward characteristics and strategic goals as the one we lightheartedly labeled our "Widow & Orphans" portfolio to distinguish it from our riskier and higher-yielding classic Income Factory.

It includes funds most of whose distributions are modest enough that they should be able to continue paying them at close to these levels indefinitely. While there are always the same risks that we have

TABLE 7.3 Income Factory Model Portfolio
(Moderate Risk/Reward—12 Funds)

Asset Class	Fund Name	Fund Symbol	Distribution Yield	Premium/ Discount
Senior Loans	Apollo Floating Rate	AFT	8.0%	−12.0%
High Yield	Credit Suisse Asset Management Income	CIK	8.5%	−9.0%
Multi-Asset	Cohen & Steers Closed End Opportunity	FOF	8.0%	−3.0%
Preferreds	First Trust Intermediate Duration Preferred & Income	FPF	7.50%	−3.0%
Convertibles	Calamos Convertible & High Income	CHY	9.3%	−3.0%
Real Estate	Nuveen Real Asset Income & Growth	JRI	7.6%	−12.0%
Utility/ Infrastructure	Cohen & Steers Infrastructure	UTF	7.3%	−5.0%
Energy & MLPs	Nuveen All Cap Energy MLP Opportunity	JMLP	12.0%	−10.0%
Finance	John Hancock Financial Opportunities	BTO	6.5%	−2.0%
Equity- Covered Call	Eaton Vance Tax-Managed Dividend Equity	ETY	8.5%	0.0%
	Cohen & Steers Global Income Builder	INB	8.5%	−7.0%
General Equity	Eaton Vance Tax Advantaged Global Dividend	ETO	9.0%	2.5%
Average			8.4%	−5.3%

articulated elsewhere, both micro and macro, given the diversification in the portfolio itself (having 12 funds) and the broad diversification within each fund, I expect this portfolio should be able to produce the river of cash we are looking for to reinvest and compound satisfactorily for many years.

Readers will recognize familiar funds from top fund management companies, including Nuveen, Cohen & Steers, Eaton Vance, John Hancock, Credit Suisse, First Trust, and Apollo.

Moderate Risk/Reward Profile—24 Funds

As we expand our moderate risk/reward portfolio to 24 funds (see Table 7.4), we increase the diversification, which should make it more attractive to larger portfolios that may not feel 12 funds provide as much diversity as they need to feel comfortable. I understand that myself, being someone who prefers to overdiversify by company, asset class, and fund manager, as I described earlier. Since our target distribution yield is now a more modest 8% to 8.5% instead of the 10% plus of our more aggressive portfolio, we can focus our selection more on asset classes and particular funds that are somewhat more conservative than the ones we use in our aggressive portfolios.

We broadened our selection in the senior secured loan segment with three well-managed funds from Nuveen (JSD), Black Rock (DSU), and Apollo (AFT), all of which have years of experience in the loan asset class. These three funds have distributions yielding in the 7% to 8% range, and as floating rate secured loans sitting at the top of the corporate capital structure, are about as recession-proof an asset class as you can find. Senior loans went through the great recession of 2008 with many healthy performing loans being marked down to bargain prices of 60 cents on the dollar. But as an asset class they performed right through the crash, and investors with well-diversified portfolios who held tight and didn't lose their nerve or sell out prematurely came through successfully (especially those who reinvested at bargain prices and yields).

Similarly with our high-yield portfolio, again packed with funds from the more modest risk end of the high-yield spectrum: Black Rock Corporate High Yield (HYT), Credit Suisse Asset Management Income (CIK), Dreyfus High Yield Strategies (DHF), and New America High Income (HYB). With distribution yields in the 7.5% to 8.5% range, these funds represent an essential asset class for carrying out our strategy. As we have pointed out elsewhere, the name "high yield" or the less respectful "junk" merely means the issuing company is rated below investment grade (i.e., rated BB+ and below) by the major rating companies like Standard & Poor's and Moody's.

TABLE 7.4 Income Factory Model Portfolio
(Moderate Risk/Reward—24 Funds)

Asset Class	Fund Name	Fund Symbol	Distribution Yield	Premium/ Discount
Senior Loans	Apollo Floating Rate	AFT	8.0%	−12.0%
	Nuveen Short Duration Credit Opps	JSD	8.0%	−8.0%
	Black Rock Debt Strategies	DSU	7.5%	−12.0%
High Yield	Credit Suisse Asset Management Income	CIK	8.5%	−9.0%
	Black Rock Corporate High Yield	HYT	8.0%	−9.0%
	Dreyfus High Yield Strategies	DHF	8.5%	−8.0%
	New America High Income	HYB	7.5%	−11.0%
Multi-Asset	Cohen & Steers Closed End Opportunity	FOF	8.0%	−3.0%
	Calamos Strategic Total Return	CSQ	7.8%	−2.0%
Preferreds	Cohen & Steers Limited Duration Preferred & Income	LDP	7.5%	−2.0%
	First Trust Intermediate Duration Preferred & Income	FPF	7.5%	−3.0%
Convertibles	Calamos Convertible & High Income	CHY	9.3%	−3.0%
Real Estate	Nuveen Real Asset Income & Growth	JRI	7.6%	−12.0%
	CBRE Clarion Global Real Estate	IGR	8.0%	−13.0%
Utility/ Infrastructure	Cohen & Steers Infrastructure	UTF	7.3%	−5.0%
	Gabelli Global Utility & Income	GLU	6.4%	−6.0%
Energy & MLPs	Nuveen All Cap Energy MLP Opportunity	JMLP	12.0%	−10.0%
Finance	First Trust Specialty Finance	FGB	9.2%	0.0%
	John Hancock Financial Opportunities	BTO	6.5%	−2.0%
Equity-Covered Call	Voya Global Advantage & Opportunity Fund	IGA	8.8%	−8.0%
	Eaton Vance Tax-Managed Dividend Equity	ETY	8.5%	0.0%
	Cohen & Steers Global Income Builder	INB	8.5%	−7.0%
General Equity	Gabelli Convertible & Income	GCV	9.4%	−4.0%
	Eaton Vance Tax Advantaged Global Dividend	ETO	9.0%	2.5%
Average			8.3%	−5.9%

What most people do not realize is that the great majority of *all* companies are rated below-investment grade or not rated at all, including virtually all the companies labeled "mid-cap" or "small-cap." That means every investor out there who owns any mid-cap or small-cap stock funds is investing in high yield or junk. The difference for those investors is that as equity owners they are actually ranked below the high-yield bondholders in the queue for payment, if the company gets into trouble. So high-yield bond investing is a step up, in terms of safety and risk management, from mid-cap or small-cap equity investing. Of course, investing in the loans of these companies, as we do in our loan fund category, is even less risky, since the loans are secured and senior to not only the bonds, but also of course to the equity down at the bottom of the ladder.

Our multi-asset category addition follows the theme of dependable, "workhorse" funds, with Calamos Strategic Total Return (CSQ) added to our old favorite Cohen & Steers Closed-End Opportunity (FOF) in this category. CSQ has an excellent record and is opportunistic in its investment mandate, holding a variety of stocks, high-yield bonds, and convertible securities. Both FOF and CSQ pay distribution yields close to our target 8% range.

In our preferreds category we added another Cohen & Steers fund, the Limited Duration Preferred & Income Fund (LDP). We have not added to our convertibles category, but are merely maintaining our existing selection, the Calamos Convertible & High Income (CHY) fund. CHY is one of those "steady Eddie" low-maintenance holdings well suited for the moderate Income Factory investor, with consistent returns and distributions going back to its inception in 2003.

In our real estate segment, we paired Nuveen Real Asset Income & Growth (JRI) with CBRE Clarion Global Real Estate (IGR). Based on their past performance, the two should provide dependable distribution yields in the mid-7% or higher range and good long-term returns.

In the utility/infrastructure category, we have two very durable and dependable funds, Cohen & Steers Infrastructure (UTF) and Gabelli Global Utility & Income (GLU).

In our energy and MLP segment, we maintain our selection from the smaller moderate risk/reward portfolio, the Nuveen All Cap Energy MLP Opportunity fund (JMLP). It currently pays an above-average distribution in the 12% range. The MLP sector has been volatile in recent years, but provides essential services and has treated its patient investors well over long periods of time.

Our finance fund choices include both candidates from our Income Factory master list that we discussed earlier: First Trust Specialty Finance (FGB) and John Hancock Financial Opportunities (BTO). Although at different ends of the spectrum, with BTO holding mostly large regional and money center banks and FGB holding business development companies (BDCs) that lend to small companies, the two funds complement each other and have both performed well over the years. FGB provides most of its return in the form of cash distributions. BTO historically has paid a smaller distribution (although still about 6.5%, modest by Income Factory standards but considered large by most of the financial community) while also providing steady appreciation because of the nature of the bank stocks it holds. As we have said before, "Job 1" in Income Factory investing is to collect that big, steady cash distribution. But we won't turn our nose up at a little capital appreciation along the way. The important thing is to know which of our investments are likely to provide which sort of return. So we should not be surprised if our generous 10% or 11% yielding funds provide little or no appreciation to go along with their rich cash payouts. Likewise, we should not be surprised if our lower-yielding funds (like BTO) don't afford us quite as much comfort and security when the market turns down, because they are not pumping out rivers of cash like our higher-yielding funds.

Finally, in our equity fund categories, we have added two additional steady performers to those already in our moderate 12-fund portfolio. In the equity-covered call segment we added Voya Global Advantage & Opportunity (IGA), yielding about 8.8% and paying attractive distributions since its inception in 2007. In the general equity category we added Gabelli Convertible & Income (GCV), which has been pumping out solid distributions since 1995.

Together, the five funds in our two equity categories are a strong lineup. From a historical perspective, Eaton Vance Tax Advantaged Global Dividend (ETO) has been a particularly strong performer, paying and sometimes even growing its cash dividends since its inception in 2004, while generating an average total return of over 10%. Because ETO has such a good record, Mr. Market sometimes prices it a bit too enthusiastically and it sells at a premium. When that happens, investors looking for a potential substitute priced more attractively may wish to consider the somewhat similarly named Eaton Vance Tax Advantaged Global Dividend Opportunities fund (ETG). Managed by the same people that run ETO, ETG also has a good long-term record, but pays a lower distribution yield in the range of 7% to 8% while typically selling at a more generous discount.

"Stretching" for Yield

Many investors may decide to stop reading right here and just get on with their investing. The basic approved list of candidate funds and the range of model portfolios we created with those funds should provide plenty of opportunity for most investors to create an Income Factory that meets their specific needs. Some may wish to just adopt one of the model portfolios as is. Others may choose to add more funds from the larger candidate list, swap out funds from the model they've chosen, or vary the weightings of each fund within the model. There is plenty of room to be creative and individualize your own Income Factory, or not.

In this chapter and the next we provide additional ideas and options for building more aggressive (souped-up) or specialized Income Factories, including (1) strategies for creating a range of more aggressive, higher risk/higher return Income Factories in this chapter and (2) model portfolios for creating an Income Factory Light portfolio and an Income Factory for taxable accounts in the following chapter.

Some investment commentators have applied the label "stretching for yield" to the strategy we are currently discussing, usually in a derisive or critical manner. We examine the thinking behind criticisms like that, to see whether they deserve to be considered conventional wisdom or just plain conventional. We employ a simplified sensitivity analysis to attempt to compare the upside potential versus the downside risk of possible aggressive strategies to help quantify the risks involved and determine whether the stretching for yield we contemplate represents a reasonable bet. Here again, we try not to let traditional mainstream views deter us from thinking outside the box, especially in ways that may enable us to squeeze more income out of our investments without incurring unreasonable risks.

* * *

Beyond the Conventional Income Factory

The Income Factory model portfolios described in Chapter 7 should provide all the average investor needs to create a portfolio with a distribution stream yielding whatever level they choose in a range of about 7.5% up to 10.5%. They can do this by replicating one of the four models, or by using the models and the base list of fund candidates, and mixing and matching to create more individualized portfolios. Any of the models can be skewed or tweaked in various ways to create higher or lower yielding portfolios, to concentrate more or less in any of the designated asset classes, or to replace or add funds to the models from the broader list of 68 fund candidates presented in Chapter 6.

For example, an investor who wanted an even more conservative portfolio than the moderate risk/reward model might choose to increase the share of some of the lower-yielding fund choices among the loans, high-yield bonds, preferreds, real estate, and utilities. Meanwhile, investors seeking a higher yield and willing to shoulder the greater risk of occasional future distribution cuts might deliberately skew their portfolio choices to some of the higher-yielding fund candidates, especially in asset classes like general equity and covered-call equity, energy and MLPs, convertibles, and multi-asset.

Table 8.1 spells out the potential impact of an investor's choices in more detail, showing what a big difference an extra 0.5% or 1%

TABLE 8.1 Growth of $1,000 Income over 30 Years

Distribution Yield	Approx. Annual Income in 30 Years	Multiple of Original $1,000
8.0%	10,000	10
8.5%	11,500	11.5
9.0%	13,000	13
9.5%	15,000	15
10.0%	17,500	17.5
10.5%	20,000	20
11.0%	23,000	23
11.5%	26,000	26
12.0%	30,000	30

(or more) in one's annual yield can make when reinvested and compounded over 30 years. A portfolio that generates $1,000 per year when invested at 8% per year grows its income to about 10 times its original amount, or $10,000 per year, in 30 years, if reinvested and compounded at that same rate. Boosting the yield by 1%, to 9%, has a compounded impact on the annual income, increasing it to $13,000 by year 30. Note that by boosting the distribution yield from 8% to 9%, which is a 12% increase in percentage yield, we end up increasing our ultimate annual income stream—30 years out—by 30%. This demonstrates how the benefit we can obtain, longer term, increases at a compounded rate from taking relatively smaller increases in risk in the present.

If we move further out the risk/reward spectrum by raising the current distribution yield from 9% to 10%, we increase our Income Factory's yearly payout from $13,000 to $17,500. That's a 35% increase in income, 30 years out, for a current increase in yield of 11% (i.e., 1% divided by 9%). The jump from 8% per year income up to 10% approximates the difference between the moderate and the aggressive risk/reward models presented in the last chapter. The ultimate difference between growing our original income level by 10 times at an

8% earnings rate versus growing it by 17 times at a 10% earnings rate explains why many investors decide it is worth making that extra effort and taking the extra risk, to achieve so much additional return.

Just to put this into further perspective, many investors purchase annuities that promise to pay them a guaranteed rate of 6% a year or thereabouts, thinking that it is safer than other investment choices. Some buy bonds or CDs at similarly low or even lower rates for the same reason. What they need to understand is that a 6% rate doubles their money only about every 12 years, or no more than about six times over 30 years, a fraction of the return they would get with an 8% or 10% yielding portfolio. So even a relatively lower yielding Income Factory that earns only 8% would grow income at almost twice the rate as that so-called safe annuity at 6%. So there is plenty of room for the Income Factory to disappoint or perform only marginally and still beat the annuity.

Thoughts on Risk, Reward, and Stretching for Yield

Many investment commentators use the term *stretching for yield* in a pretty disdainful manner, suggesting that high-yielding securities are, by their nature, inherently dangerous and should be avoided by prudent investors. The assumption they make is that high yields are somehow "abnormal" and always indicate some underlying problem lurking in the shadows (or maybe even in the open) that will derail the issuer's ability to make the distribution payment you are counting on.

It is apparent from many of the comments to articles I have written on this subject that lots of investors have bought into this "high yields always equal danger" refrain. But I hope readers keep an open mind as we examine the proposition more closely.

The term *high yield* does not mean the same thing in all markets or asset classes. A yield that may be relatively high and represent a serious risk in one asset class may be much more typical and "normal" in another. In the corporate stock market, a typical healthy industrial company may pay a dividend yield in the range of 2% to 4%. And then it is expected to grow its earnings and dividend by another 5% to 8%, for a total return of more or less 10%. In the world of corporate stocks, when you see a company paying a dividend of 6%, 7%, or higher, unless it is in an industry where that is the norm, it may indeed signal trouble of some kind. It may mean that the company's growth prospects have slowed down and the rich dividend is about all stockholders can ever expect. Mr. Market, recognizing that, will have priced the company's stock down to a point that reflects its low or nonexistent growth prospects.

An atypically high corporate dividend can also be signaling something else. It may mean the market has determined that the dividend payment is in jeopardy and carries a high likelihood of being reduced or cut out completely. In that case, the market may have already reduced the price to the level it considers will be a reasonable percentage yield after the anticipated dividend cut takes place. For example, suppose a company pays a dividend of $4 per year and sells for $100 per share. That $4 dividend represents a 4% yield on the $100 share price. Suppose over time the price drops down to $50 per share. As long as the company continues to pay its $4 dividend, then its new yield is 4 divided by 50, or 8%. That 8% yield may seem awfully attractive, but if in fact it merely means the market has correctly determined the dividend is due to be cut, then the high yield may be sending a false signal to investors who take it at face value.

In both cases, either where a company's unusually high dividend yield reflects stagnant growth prospects or where it signals an impending dividend cut, the high yield is suspect and not to be relied upon.

But there are other asset classes where higher yields are normal and to be expected, and are not suspect or harbingers of doom. These are the asset classes we want to identify and use in our Income Factory, all of which we have mentioned already. They include:

- Utilities and infrastructure companies with predictable growth paths and revenue projections, where the financial markets expect them to pay out most of their earnings in the form of

dividends, and higher-than-normal dividend yields are to be
expected and are not a negative indicator

- Master limited partnerships (MLPs) and business development
  corporations (BDCs), both of which were designed specifically
  to pay higher distributions, with tax and regulatory requirements that mandate them to pay out most or all of their cash
  flows to their shareholders
- Specialized vehicles, like collateralized loan obligations, that
  hold senior, secured corporate loans and use low-cost leverage to
  generate high cash flows for investors
- High-yield debt, like loans and bonds to non-investment grade
  companies, where, by definition, the entire return to investors is
  in the form of relatively high-yielding interest payments
- Closed-end funds in general, which are designed to be income
  vehicles and where many of them use leverage, options, and
  other strategies to pay distributions higher than what the underlying assets they hold would be able to pay if held directly. Like
  MLPs and BDCs, closed-end funds have a similar feature where
  the earnings are not taxed at the fund level but "pass through"
  to be taxed at the investor level

Obviously, we have to do proper due diligence on everything we
add to our portfolio, but it is important to recognize that a high dividend, in and of itself, does not automatically indicate danger or undue
risk, as many investors have been taught or led to believe.

Closed-End Funds: Income Boosters

Closed-end funds, in particular, have two additional advantages,
which is why I use them as the investment vehicle of choice for implementing my Income Factory strategy. First of all, they are traded on
the open market and not issued and redeemed directly by a fund
company like typical open-end mutual funds. As a result, the market
value of a closed-end fund varies, on a continual basis, from the exact
underlying value of the net assets that make up the fund. That means,
if you time your purchases appropriately, you can buy most closed-end

funds at a discount to their actual net asset value (NAV). That means a fund whose underlying assets may be worth $10 per share might—on occasion—be selling for $9. That 10% discount means that an investor will have $10 of assets working for them that they only had to pay $9 for. If the $10 in assets were yielding, say, 8% (i.e., 80 cents per share), then by only paying $9, you are actually getting a yield of 80 cents divided by $9, which equals 8.9%, rather than the 8% you would be earning if you paid full price. As already discussed, collecting that extra 0.9% makes a big difference over many decades of investing.

The other attractive feature of closed-end funds is their ability to leverage themselves at low-cost institutional borrowing rates. This means a closed-end fund can issue debt up to 50% of the amount of its equity (i.e., its debt can never exceed one-third of the total value of the fund's assets). For example, a fund investing in high-yield bonds paying interest of 8% might go out and borrow up to 50% of the amount of its existing equity at, say, 3%, and invest it in additional high-yield bonds at 8%. The spread between its cost of leverage and the earnings on its assets would be 8% minus 3%, for a spread of 5%. That additional spread would accrue to the benefit of the fund's shareholders. Since the fund is limited to leveraging itself by only 50% of the amount of its equity, each shareholder would only get the benefit of half of the additional spread, on a pro rata basis. That would be half of 5%, or 2.5%, if the fund were fully leveraged to its maximum limit. Most funds don't go all the way to their limits, since they don't want to risk exceeding the limit if the market price of their assets were to drop. So in our example, the average additional spread might more likely be only 1.5% to 2% or thereabouts. The point is that leverage is a powerful way to enable shareholders to be paid a yield that is greater than what the natural yield of the underlying fund assets would be.

When you combine these two features—buying at a discount and having extra assets that you didn't have to pay for but are working for you, along with leveraging your earning assets with cheap borrowed money—a closed-end fund may end up being able to pay its shareholders a distribution yield of 9% or 10% even when the assets it holds generate an underlying yield of only 6% or 7%.

Once you understand where that higher yield is coming from, that it is a logical result of the underlying asset class's normal rate of return, with the added benefit of discount pricing and modest low-priced leverage, then the resulting high yield is not so hard to understand, nor does it present particularly daunting risks.

Stretching for Even More Yield

Up until now, we have presented our Income Factory risk/reward choices within a spectrum ranging from moderate, which we defined as plus or minus 8% distribution yields, to aggressive, which is how we have described the 10% to 10.5% yield range. Through the use of our model portfolios, or by making choices from our Income Factory candidates list or from one's own research, investors can create portfolios anywhere on the scale between just below 8% yields to somewhere up in the 11% yield range, which should accommodate most Income Factory investors.

But there are investors (like myself) who are willing to go even further out on the risk/reward limb to boost their Income Factory output. The reason we do this is the familiar reason we have been emphasizing consistently right along. A relatively small increase in yield, if reinvested and compounded over the long term, can make a big difference in how much our income grows over 20 or 30 years. As we saw in Table 8.1, increasing our average reinvested distribution yield from 8% to 9% or 10% results in a substantial jump in the income we end up with 30 years later. Moving into higher-yielding territory pays off with even more substantial income growth later on, for investors with a higher risk/reward tolerance level.

One of the ways we can help manage risk/reward concerns is to keep them in perspective. I find it useful to do a simple sensitivity analysis like that shown in Table 8.2, where we compare the amount of additional income to be gained from moving up the distribution yield scale (i.e., stretching for yield, as some might call it), to what a reasonable downside result might be if the extra yield fails to materialize.

TABLE 8.2 Impact of Souping Up Our Income Factory

Shows How Adding Higher Risk/Reward Assets Affects Overall Yield of "Base" Income Factory			Downside Case: Souping Up Fails
Yield of Base Income Factory	% of Higher Yielding 15% Assets Added to Base	Yield of Souped-Up Income Factory	Yield of Souped-Down Income Factory
10%	0%	10.0%	10.0%
10%	5%	10.3%	9.9%
10%	10%	10.5%	9.8%
10%	15%	10.8%	9.6%
10%	20%	11.0%	9.5%
10%	25%	11.3%	9.4%
10%	30%	11.5%	9.3%
10%	35%	11.8%	9.1%
10%	40%	12.0%	9.0%
10%	45%	12.3%	8.9%
10%	50%	12.5%	8.8%
Yield on Souped-Up Assets:		15.0% (Best Case)	7.5% (Draconian Case)

In Table 8.2 we start with an Income Factory that is already invested in a portfolio with distribution yields averaging 10%. The table shows what the average portfolio yield would increase to if we souped it up with varying amounts of ultra-high-yielding assets averaging 15%. We also show what the impact on our overall portfolio would be if our ultra-high yielders failed to deliver the expected yields and, in fact, slashed their yields by 50%, to 7.5%. This seems like a reasonably draconian scenario since whatever ultra-high-yielding assets we chose would be diversified funds where, even if the distribution were cut, it would most likely merely be decreased, perhaps substantially, but not eliminated. That, as we pointed out previously, is the big difference between holding funds, which by nature are diversified, and individual corporate stocks, where if trouble strikes, the entire dividend may be at risk instead of just a small portion of a pool of separate issuers.

To take one example from Table 8.2, suppose we start with our portfolio that averages 10% average distribution yields and replace 20% of it with ultra-high-yielding funds averaging 15% yields. That would take the entire portfolio's average yield up to 11% per annum. As we saw back in Table 8.1, that's a rate at which our annual income over 30 years grows to be about 23 times the amount we start with, versus only about 17 times as much if compounded at a 10% annual rate.

Most of us would probably agree that growing our projected 30-year annual income by 23 times versus 17 times its original amount is worth taking some risk for, as long as the risk is reasonable. In evaluating what is "reasonable," we have to consider what would or could likely go wrong with such a strategy. In my view, projecting a 50% drop in income from a diversified fund is pretty draconian, although it still depends on what sort of assets our fund holds. In general, such a drop would require half the assets in the fund to completely cease whatever sort of payment it was (interest, dividend, etc.) that they were previously making. Given that default rates in the high-yield loan and bond market (to take one obvious high-yield category) never reached higher than 12% during the worst of the financial crisis of 2008, the probability of a 50% cut in payments from whatever ultra-high-yielding funds we select seems pretty remote.

But in our example (a 10% base rate portfolio boosted by replacing 20% of its assets with ultra-high-yielding 15% assets), even if we assume a 50% drop in income from those ultra-high-yielding assets (from 15% down to 7.5%), the impact on our overall Income Factory would be to reduce the portfolio yield to 9.5%, only 0.5% lower than the original 10% distribution we started with.

My personal assets of choice for executing an ultra-high-yield strategy are closed-end funds that hold collateralized loan obligations (CLOs). The two most widely held closed-end funds in this category are Eagle Point Credit (ECC) and Oxford Lane Capital (OXLC), which pay distribution yields, respectively, of about 13% and 16%. ECC and OXLC are good examples of funds whose yields are driven higher than they probably deserve to be, from a pure credit risk standpoint, because of their perceived complexity risk. The two funds own equity in CLOs, which are securitized vehicles that hold senior secured corporate loans to major multinational corporations. While CLOs are complex and challenging for many investors to understand, they are well diversified with loans that are highly transparent and generally well secured. Equally important, they are a type of investment security with an excellent record of holding up well through difficult markets, having come through the great recession and financial crash of 2008 very strongly for investors who held tight and just collected their interest and dividend payments. So they are a classic case of an asset class whose yields are driven up because of complexity risk more than fundamental credit risk. As such, they are a good fit for an Income Factory strategy like ours that values consistent cash generation over market price stability and/or appreciation. (See Chapter 13 for a more detailed look at the structure, risks, and rewards of CLOs.)

If we replaced just 10% of our base portfolio with an equal amount of each of these two funds, which is a more conservative example than the one previously described, it would raise the overall blended portfolio yield by 0.5%, to 10.5%. That additional 0.5%, compounded over 30 years, would raise our projected income to about 20 times its original level, versus about 17 times at a compounding rate of 10%. However, if the distributions were cut by 50%, which seems highly unlikely, the yield on the portfolio would only drop to 9.75%, a mere 0.25% below its starting point and still a highly respectable long-term equity return.

If we wanted to adopt the more aggressive strategy described earlier, where we replace 20% of our portfolio's existing assets with ultra-high-yielding ones, ECC and OXLC would be good candidates to start with. But we might wish to use other high-yielding funds as well, just to avoid having a single fund account for as much as 10% of our portfolio income. Readers may wish to consider funds in the energy/resource/MLP sector, which is a prime recent example of an industry whose cash-flow prospects appear to be undiminished despite a continuing lag in their market price performance. Other ultra-high or above-average yield candidates include the leveraged exchange-traded notes issued by UBS (https://etracs.ubs.com/) and Credit Suisse (https://notes.credit-suisse.com/etn/index.html). These notes involve essentially leveraged bets on various asset classes and generally offer distribution yields in the mid-teens and higher. Fortunately they are actively covered on investment sites like Seeking Alpha, and investors should thoroughly research them before making any purchase decisions.

In general, finding ultra-high-yielding assets that are reasonable candidates for our Income Factories means being opportunistic about which asset classes are at low points or out of favor with the market at any particular time. In the closed-end fund world, the CEF Connect site (www.cefconnect.com) is a good source for finding fund candidates that allows you to search by industry, yield, premium/discount, and various performance metrics. (Links to learn about other Income Factory candidates are included in Chapter 1.)

As we saw earlier, the downside risk incurred in stretching for this additional return (i.e., the yield we sacrifice if our ultra-high-yield strategy fails) appears to be about half as much as our upside potential (the yield we gain if our ultra-high-yielding assets maintain their payouts), and in both cases the resulting yields, even in failed outcomes, are highly respectable long-term returns.

Is ratcheting up our risk/reward like this necessary to a successful Income Factory strategy? Obviously not, since by now I hope we have demonstrated that any number of Income Factory strategies and outcomes, ranging from returns of 8% through 10% or 11% and higher, are all satisfactory long-term outcomes. More important, they are all better outcomes than the typical investor obtains from annuities, from traditional "balanced" portfolios that use low-yielding assets as hedges or anchors, or from just moving to the sidelines occasionally to avoid stressful periods of market volatility. Our goal is to show how a variety of Income Factory strategies—conservative, moderate, aggressive, or hyper-aggressive—are all possible and can fit the risk/reward profile and investing style and temperament of a whole range of investors. The one thing all the strategies have in common is their reliance

on high cash distributions, reinvestment, and compounding to produce their long-term growth, rather than depending on the growth of
earnings, distributions, or market price.

That is the essence of the Income Factory philosophy, that "math
is math" and we can achieve any particular total return by whatever
combination of dividend yield and price appreciation or depreciation
adds up to that number. In other words, a 10% yield plus zero growth
in market price equals a total return of 10% just as much as a zero
dividend yield and 10% market price growth, or 5% dividend yield
and 5% growth. This should not seem like a radical concept, but, of
course, it was when I first introduced it several years ago in my articles on the Seeking Alpha site. As many readers and investors have
already realized, we do not have to be slaves to an investment doctrine
that requires earnings or market price growth, but can achieve all the
growth any long-term investor needs through collecting distributions,
and reinvesting and compounding them.

Once readers understand that principle, they are free to create their
own Income Factories with whatever types of assets—modest yield,
high yield, ultra-high yield—they are comfortable with. It isn't the
type of assets selected, per se, that makes it an Income Factory, but
rather the attitude and intention that goes along with it. I hope investors will view all these models and additional ideas for tweaking or
souping them up as tools to empower them to be as creative as possible in applying the Income Factory philosophy to their own personal
circumstances.

Variations on
the Theme

We noted that some investors may be intrigued by the Income Factory philosophy but are not prepared to go the "Full Monty" and completely give up traditional strategies that rely on increases in earnings, dividends, and stock prices as their primary long-term engine of growth.

At the same time, they realize that fully executing a long-term total return strategy requires the personal discipline to stay calm and resist the temptation to sell out during downturns. This is where the high current cash output of an Income Factory can be a big help in stiffening one's upper lip at times of market turmoil.

In this chapter, for those investors who want it both ways, we introduce the Income Factory Light (IFL), which combines the elements of a traditional dividend growth investing (DGI) strategy with those of an Income Factory, and hopefully, provides the essentials of both (1) a current river of cash sufficient to fend off the temptation to "head for the hills" that engulfs so many investors when they see markets dropping all around them along with (2) a portfolio of investments with enough potential earnings and dividend growth to make up the difference between an IFL's somewhat lighter-than-normal distribution yield and the expected 8% to 10% or higher-equity return goal that most of us are targeting.

In addition, we also address the unique challenges facing investors who want to use an Income Factory strategy in a taxable account. The key there is to try to find investment candidates—stocks or funds—that offer high but durable yields, and which are untaxed, tax-deferred, or taxed at low rates (i.e., qualified dividends or equivalent). Many of the stocks or funds that might be appropriate for an IFL portfolio probably pay qualified dividends, so they may also be suitable candidates for a taxable Income Factory.

*   *   *

Income Factory Light

As discussed earlier, the appeal of an Income Factory strategy can be emotional and psychological as well as purely economic and financial. There are many paths to a long-term equity return, which we have defined, based on the historical record over the past century, as somewhere in the range of 8% to 10%. But even a return in the 8% range, which is the target for our more moderate risk/reward model portfolios, is still well above what a typical investor achieves over the long run. That's because they often move in and out of the market in an attempt to time its upward and downward movements, or they hedge or diversify by buying bonds or other securities that drag down overall results by locking in substandard returns in an effort to limit temporary or paper losses.

So one of the main attractions of the Income Factory approach is *not* that it will earn *more* than other traditional investment strategies whose goal is the same equity return of 8% or 10%. The attraction is that it can make that goal easier to achieve for many investors because its high current cash income stream gives investors a greater sense of control over their own investment destiny, insulating them from some of the angst and stress that can lead to poor short-term decisions. During market downturns and bear markets especially, while many typical investors are wringing their hands as they watch their stocks drop in price, Income Factory investors can collect and reinvest their high cash dividends at bargain prices and abnormally high yields. Knowing your income is growing faster than ever because market prices are dropping adds a whole new perspective—a positive one—to market pullbacks, making it easier to ignore negative and overly reactive media and market commentary.

Investors who want both the warm, fuzzy feeling the high current cash payments from an Income Factory give them, and the promise of long-term growth of their earnings, dividends, and stock prices can get a blend with an IFL strategy. In an IFL, we blend some traditional DGI stocks with a conventional Income Factory portfolio. Our goal is to achieve a current dividend yield high enough to provide a sense of security during market downturns without giving up the opportunity to achieve more traditional earnings and market price growth. Back in Chapter 5 we presented a broad range of possible combinations of dividend growth stocks and Income Factory funds (Table 5.3) showing how investors could mix and match various proportions and different risk/reward profiles to achieve IFL strategies that run the gamut from 6% yields to over 10%. In this chapter we get a bit more specific in terms of model portfolios, but investors should remember that they can be as flexible and creative as they want in creating an IFL that works for them.

Most investors who are considering an IFL strategy already have their own portfolios of favorite dividend growth stocks, lists of approved candidates, or both, and they can come up with many more prospects by merely searching online for "dividend growth stocks," "dividend champions," or similar phrases. But anyone without an existing portfolio who would like to create an IFL portfolio easily without having to do it totally from scratch, may wish to consider Table 9.1, which contains a starter list of dividend growth stock candidates from popular sources that could be used as a base for a blended Income Factory/dividend growth stock portfolio. The 17 stocks listed are all long-time dividend payers with yields mostly in the 4% to 6% range, although some of the energy stocks, which have been depressed

TABLE 9.1 DGI Candidates for IFL

Name	Symbol	Dividend Yield
Brixmor Property	BRX	5.4%
Occidental Petroleum	OXY	7.8%
AT&T	T	5.3%
Kimco Realty	KIM	5.4%
BP	BP	6.6%
Royal Dutch Shell	RDSB	6.5%
Helmerich & Payne	HP	7.8%
PPL Corp.	PPL	5.2%
Simon Property	SPG	5.6%
Dominion Energy	D	4.5%
IBM	IBM	4.8%
Ventas	VTR	4.5%
TransCanada	TRP	4.5%
Southern Co	SO	4.1%
Verizon	VZ	4.0%
Legg Mason	LM	4.5%
Duke Energy	DUK	4.0%
Average Yield		**5.3%**

lately, have yields that are somewhat higher. The average yield, if one were to hold all of them in equal proportion, is slightly above 5%. This puts them at the higher-yielding end, but still solidly within, the definition of a typical dividend growth stock. That means they have the twin hallmarks of the dividend growth investing universe: a history of steadily increasing earnings and dividend payments, and an expectation of continued future growth.

IFL Models

In Table 9.2 we introduce a "do-it-yourself kit" approach that uses existing portfolio building blocks we have already introduced. It shows a simple matrix of four different possible IFL models, each using a blend of dividend growth stocks from Table 9.1 and funds from one of the 12-fund Income Factory models presented back in Chapter 7.

TABLE 9.2 IFL "Do-It-Yourself Kit" Models
(Blend of Income Factory & DGI)

Source of the Income Factory Portion of the Blend	Percentage in Income Factory	Percentage in DGI Portfolio	Average Yield in IF	Average Yield in DGI	Blended Yield
Income Factory Funds from Aggressive Risk/ Reward 12 Funds Model from Table 7.1	75%	25%	10.3%	5.3%	9.0%
	50%	50%	10.3%	5.3%	7.8%
Income Factory Funds from Moderate Risk/ Reward 12 Funds Model from Table 7.3	75%	25%	8.4%	5.3%	7.6%
	50%	50%	8.4%	5.3%	6.8%

The first two lines of Table 9.2 assume you build your IFL with a combination of the funds from the aggressive risk/reward—12 funds model (from Table 7.1) and the dividend growth (DGI) stocks from Table 9.1. Using those two portfolio sources, the first line shows how you could create an IFL that yields 9% with a blended portfolio sourced 75% from the Income Factory model and 25% from the dividend growth stocks. Obviously, such a strategy would be mostly Income Factory with the dividend growth stocks playing a smaller but not inconsequential part in it. Looking at the math, we assume an entire portfolio of dividend growth stocks yielding 5% would be expected to grow their dividends at the rate of about 5% to get their total return up to 10%. So using such stocks for 25% of our portfolio might be expected to add another 1.25% to the entire portfolio's total return (i.e., 25% times 5% = 1.25%). So the total expected return from this blended portfolio would be its distribution yield of 9% plus the additional "growth return" of 1.25%, bringing the total projected return up to a very attractive equity return of 10.25%. The strategy is mostly an Income Factory approach, with dividend growth being the icing on the cake.

The second line of Table 9.2 assumes the use of the same invest-ment sources but with a 50-50 split from each source. So this IFL represents a true partnership between the two strategies. In this case we end up with a lower current distribution yield of 7.8%, which is at the bottom of the range we would consider a full-fledged Income Factory return. But that should still provide enough of a river of cash to stiffen most investors' spines through market downturns. Along with doing that, the 50% of the portfolio invested in dividend growth stocks is expected to provide perhaps another 5% of long-term growth for its half of the portfolio, or 2.5% for the portfolio as a whole. That 2.5% growth boost plus the 7.8% distribution yield again brings the overall total return to about 10.3%.

Both models, the first one skewed more toward the Income Factory and the second one balanced 50-50, result in virtually the same equity return. I imagine the 50-50 model might be attractive to many inves-tors who seek an equity return and the comfort of a high-dividend stream, but are still nervous about embracing either alternative—100% dividend growth stocks, or 100% high-yield Income Factory assets—in its entirety.

Lines 3 and 4 in Table 9.2 represent a more conservative approach, where we blend the moderate risk/reward—12 funds model from Table 7.3 with the dividend-growth candidates from Table 9.1. In the 75%/25% portfolio, using the lower risk/reward profile Income Fac-tory investments (with their average distribution yield of 8.4%) results in the model having a projected overall yield of 7.6%. When you add in the additional 1.25% expected growth from the dividend growth stocks' 25% of the portfolio, the projected total return is about 8.85%. As discussed earlier, that is quite a reasonable long-term return, one that provides consistent cash income buildup without sacrificing some of the benefits many investors perceive in a growth-oriented strategy.

The moderate 50-50 strategy (line 4 in the table), provides even more of that potential equity growth satisfaction for investors who want it, while still maintaining an Income Factory anchor for those more volatile periods. The yield on the 50-50 blended IFL is 6.8%, the bare minimum river of cash we might want. But when you add to it the projected 2.5% of additional return expected from the dividend growth stocks' expected (hoped for) capital appreciation, the overall Factory's total return could exceed 9%. Most conservative investors would probably be quite satisfied with that long-term result.

All of these blended combinations of Income Factory and DGI styles seem to achieve both of the twin objectives: achieving an equity total return close to 9% or higher, and collecting enough of it in current cash (close to 7% or more) to provide both a financial and emotional buffer during periods of market turmoil.

Income Factories in Taxable Accounts

As noted earlier, tax-deferred Individual Retirement Accounts (IRAs) are ideal vehicles for Income Factory investing because you can tweak your investment portfolio, buy and sell, replace assets, and—most important—reinvest and compound your cash distributions all you want and never have any "leakage" to pay taxes until decades later when you have to begin mandatory distributions. Even better is a Roth IRA, where you don't even have to pay any taxes later on when you take out distributions. But a regular IRA (which is what the author has) still allows you years and years of tax-deferred "inside buildup" to achieve the sort of growth that the examples in the various tables have presented.

Tax-deferred vehicles have another advantage in that you don't have to worry so much about the nature of the dividends and distributions you are receiving, reinvesting, and compounding inside your Income Factory. Whether they consist of qualified dividends that get taxed at a lower rate, or regular income like interest that gets taxed at normal tax rates, or some form of return of capital that represents your own principal and is not taxed (but may lower your cost basis and affect your future capital gain or loss), none of that matters much to you if you are receiving and reinvesting it inside a tax-deferred vehicle. That's because later on, when you take distributions from the IRA or whatever sort of tax-deferred vehicle it happens to be, they will all be taxed at your ordinary income tax rate, regardless of how those payments were originally categorized when paid as distributions within the IRA (unless, of course, they are in a Roth IRA whose distributions are tax free).

But for those investors who want to adopt an Income Factory strategy in taxable accounts, there are still options for minimizing the tax impact and maximizing the inside buildup from reinvestment and compounding. Back in Chapter 5 we compared the returns over time between a tax-deferred Income Factory and one that was a taxable account. We saw that a 10% yielding tax-deferred Income Factory became, effectively, an 8.5% yielding Income Factory if we successfully managed to ensure that 100% of its investments paid qualified dividends that would only be taxed at a 15% rate.

The difference between the two rates of return, as shown in Table 5.1, was that the tax-deferred IRA doubled and redoubled its income stream almost every 7 years, while the taxable Income Factory's output doubled and redoubled about every 8.5 years. Those are both satisfactory long-term results, but the IRA lengthens its lead, as we would expect from the other examples already cited, quite substantially 30 and 40 years out. To minimize the tax drag on a taxable Income Factory's performance, it is important to try to choose funds or other assets that pay qualified dividends that are eligible for the lower tax rate (which is also the capital gains tax rate) of 15% for those with incomes up to about $425,000. Incomes higher than that amount incur a capital gains/qualified dividend tax rate of 20%.

Fortunately, the closed-end fund universe includes a category of funds that label themselves "tax advantaged" and are managed by respected fund managers like Eaton Vance, Nuveen, John Hancock, Gabelli, and others. These funds make a special effort to invest in stocks whose dividends fall into the qualified dividend category. Beyond the specifically labeled tax-advantaged funds, many funds in the general equity and other categories go beyond just providing distributions that are qualified and eligible for the lower tax rate. These funds may deliberately attempt or be required by law to pay part of their distribution in the form of what is called a return of capital (ROC) and is therefore not taxable as income in the current period. Return of capital is treated as a reduction in the investor's cost basis of the fund, so it increases the capital gain (or reduces the capital loss) that an investor realizes and pays taxes on sometime later (possibly many years later) when they eventually sell their shares in the fund.

Return of capital is a much misunderstood term in the closed-end fund world and often has a negative connotation, as if the distribution is not somehow real or justified. If used prudently, returns of capital allow funds to tap into the unrealized appreciation of stocks on their balance sheets that have gone up since the fund bought them. And they essentially distribute some of that increased value (which is very real) to fund holders even though the fund has not yet sold the appreciated stocks or realized the capital gain. The as yet unrealized gain is part of the fund's accounting income but not (since they have not yet sold the appreciated stock) a part of its taxable income. This type of ROC is often referred to as constructive as opposed to destructive because it represents the fund's monetizing real income, the unrealized gain—that is, distributing it, using funds from other sources—without actually liquidating the specific stocks that have gone up in value.

Monetizing and paying out to shareholders real profits that just haven't been realized yet is considered constructive. But paying out money that hasn't actually been earned and represents a diminution in the value of a shareholder's investment is considered destructive. A continuing policy of paying out constructive return of capital is healthy for a fund and its investors, especially if the investors hold the fund shares in a taxable account and defer taxes as a result. However, paying out a destructive dividend on a continuing basis eventually erodes the value of the investment down to zero.

If it all sounds complicated, that's because it can be, although some of the fund companies, especially Nuveen and Eaton Vance, have done a good job on their websites of explaining the difference between constructive and destructive ROC. In a nutshell, if a fund is paying out to its shareholders more than it is actually earning over time, and its net asset value drops steadily over the same time period, then the ROC is almost undoubtedly destructive. If its dividend—from whatever sources—is being covered by the fund's earnings, from whatever sources, then it's not destructive. This is an important issue and needs to be monitored closely, regardless of whether we are investing in a taxable or tax-deferred Income Factory.

TABLE 9.3 Income Factory Model Portfolio—Taxable Account

Asset Class	Fund/Security Name	Symbol	Distribution Yield	Premium/ Discount
Tax Advantaged Equity	Eaton Vance Tax Advantaged Global Dividend Opportunity	ETO	8.9%	3.0%
	Nuveen Tax Advantaged Total Return	JTA	8.4%	-5.0%
	Nuveen Tax Advantaged Dividend Growth	JTD	7.5%	-2.0%
	Eaton Vance Tax Advantaged Global Dividend Income	ETG	7.7%	-7.0%
Equity- Covered Call	Guggenheim Enhanced Equity Income	GPM	11.8%	3.4%
	Eaton Vance Risk Managed Diversified Equity Income	ETJ	9.7%	0.0%
	Cohen & Steers Global Income Builder	INB	8.6%	-6.0%
	Eaton Vance Managed Buy- Write Strategy	EXD	9.0%	-7.0%
General Equity	Liberty All-Star Equity	USA	10.6%	-4.0%
	Gabelli Equity Trust	GAB	9.7%	6.0%
	Gabelli Convertible & Income	GCV	9.4%	-4.0%
Energy & MLPs	Fiduciary Claymore Energy Infrastructure	FMO	13.5%	-7.0%
	Nuveen All Cap Energy MLP Opportunity	JMLP	12.0%	-10.0%
	Tortoise Energy Infrastructure	TYG	11.6%	-3.0%
Average			9.9%	-2.8%

Table 9.3 presents our Income Factory model portfolio for a taxable account. There are essentially four types of funds included, all of which pay distributions that are mostly either qualified dividends and capital gains (both of which are taxed at the capital gains tax rate of 15%, or for higher income, 20%), or that distribute substantial amounts of constructive ROC, which defers taxes until the funds are sold:

- Equity tax advantaged funds
- Equity-covered call funds
- General equity funds
- Master limited partnership (MLP) funds

In addition to these, investors may wish to consider adding stocks from our DGI candidates list (Table 9.1). Since the 15% or 20% taxes that we have to pay in a taxable account become a drag on the reinvesting and compounding that we count on as an essential feature of an Income Factory, we can offset some of that over time if we allocate some of our portfolio to securities that are expected to generate capital appreciation along with their current dividends. The capital appreciation, of course, won't be taxed until it is realized at sale, which may come years later.

In short, a taxable Income Factory is a good candidate to also be an IFL, and vice versa. This is largely because the sort of DGI stocks that combine modest current dividend payments with the prospect of longer-term growth in earnings, dividends, and stock prices also tend to be the same kind of stocks that generate qualified dividends for tax purposes.

Our taxable Income Factory model (Table 9.3) presents a pure Income Factory, with a distribution yield (before taxes) of almost 10% annually, providing sufficient cash flow to reinvest and compound for a long-term equity return, even after current taxes are paid on the distributions. In Table 9.4 we show what happens when a selection of DGI stocks like those listed in Table 9.1 is added to the portfolio in a sufficient amount to bring the proportion of DGI stocks to 25% of the entire portfolio.

TABLE 9.4 Taxable IFL—Model Portfolio (75-25) Split

Asset Class	% of Portfolio	Source of Investments	Average Yield of Funds/Stocks
Closed-End Funds	75%	Income Factory—Model Portfolio—Taxable Account (Table 9.3)	10%
Dividend Growth Stocks	25%	Dividend Growth Candidates for IFL (Table 9.1)	5%
Weighted Average Yield of Blended Portfolio			8.75%

Doing that brings the weighted average yield on what now becomes a taxable IFL, down to 8.75%, from its previous level (before the DGI stocks were added) of 10%. But the offsetting upside is that we have added stocks that have the potential to grow by an additional 5% or so per annum, whose growth is not taxed until the stocks are sold and the gain is realized. If the stocks do achieve the anticipated 5% growth, the additional impact on the portfolio as a whole is about 1.25% (i.e., 25% times 5%). So the total anticipated return becomes the yield (8.75%), which is taxable, plus the additional growth of 1.25% per annum, which may be deferred indefinitely until the assets are sold and the appreciation is realized.

In Table 9.5 we increase the proportion of stock from our DGI portfolio to 50%, so the split between the basic taxable Income Factory from Table 9.3 and our DGI stock portfolio is now balanced at 50-50. This has the impact of reducing the overall weighted yield to about 7.5%, but it also means that half the portfolio now consists of stocks that have upside appreciation potential that can be deferred until it is realized, in addition to the cash dividend yields.

TABLE 9.5 Taxable IFL—Model Portfolio (50-50) Split

Asset Class	% of Portfolio	Source of Investments	Average Yield of Funds/Stocks
Closed-End Funds	50%	Income Factory—Model Portfolio—Taxable Account (Table 9.3)	10%
Dividend Growth Stocks	50%	Dividend Growth Candidates for IFL (Table 9.1)	5%
Weighted Average Yield of Blended Portfolio			7.5%

That could add another 2.5% or more per annum (depending, of course, on how much growth our dividend growth stocks actually provide over many years) to this IFL's overall long-term total return. This could be a very attractive solution to taxable investors who see the value of having a strong current cash flow to comfort them through the rough spots (even though it will be taxed), but basically do not want to completely abandon a traditional DGI strategy, with the possibility of long-term, tax-deferred gains.

We should caution readers, once again, that all these projected yields and returns, here and throughout the book, are intended to be illustrative and approximate, since real market prices and yields, for the funds and the stocks listed, are a moving target that changes regularly. That is why we will be updating our models and candidate lists from time to time in our Seeking Alpha blog posts and articles, with the link listed in Chapter 1, or just search online for the author's name or "Income Factory." We also urge you to not just accept my opinion about all this, but to do as much of your own research and due diligence as possible. That is doubly true about tax laws and their application to anyone's personal Income Factory, where the treatment of tax issues described here is of a very general nature and should not be relied upon as "tax advice."

The Taxonomy of Risk and Reward

One of the main themes of our earlier chapters was that investors can earn an equity return without actually owning equity by focusing on fixed-income investments instead of stocks. But we define *fixed income* a bit more broadly than is the norm, including not only traditional debt instruments like bonds, loans, and preferred stock, but also stock and other asset classes that provide most or all of their equity return through steady dividends or distributions.

Our strategy rests on the underlying assumption that credit risk, if undertaken in broadly diversified portfolios, is more easily modeled and projected than stock market volatility. Hence, a strategy based on taking credit risk rather than equity risk may allow investors fewer sleepless nights over time and offer less temptation, when markets experience turbulent conditions, to take defensive actions they might regret later.

In the next few chapters we deconstruct the risks and rewards of the major asset classes (equities and various credit investments) that we consider candidates for our Income Factory. We describe how if you dissect the yield of virtually all investments, you find "layers of compensation" for four different services provided or risks taken by the investors: (1) a "risk free" rate, (2) interest rate risk, (3) credit risk, and (4) equity risk.

We also explore a key insight underpinning our Income Factory philosophy. It is the idea that equity investors, besides taking on the entrepreneurial risk and reward of owning a company, also take on the firm's credit risk, every bit as much as its debt holders.

That means purchase of a company's stock isn't worth considering unless we can expect to earn a higher total return than the interest rate we would receive if we merely bought the company's debt. Fortunately for equity investors, common stock total returns have historically averaged in the range of 8% to 10% per annum, about 3% higher than the interest rate investors have received recently on corporate debt (high-yield bonds and corporate bank loans). One of our key strategies, as Income Factory investors, is to find ways to close that 3% gap and earn the full equity return, but by confining ourselves to less volatile fixed-income securities.

*   *   *

Fixed Income and Our Income Factory

Our Income Factory strategy depends heavily on high-yielding, fixed-income investments, since its entire premise is that we do not require or even expect our individual securities to grow (either their earnings and dividends, or their market price). Instead, we are happy as long as (1) they pay us a distribution yield high enough to constitute what would be regarded historically as an equity return of 8% to 10%, and (2) equally important, that they can sustain that level of distribution consistently into the future. As long as we can count on getting a high, steady cash flow from our investment, we don't have to worry about whether the security itself grows or not, since we can create our own growth through reinvesting and compounding.

Our fixed-income investments essentially involve bets on a company's staying in business and continuing its current level of performance. That means not only paying its bills and meeting its current interest and principal payments, but also paying its current level of dividends or other distributions. We are not betting on or anticipating that a company will grow its sales, increase its earnings or dividend payments, or expand its overall business enterprise to the degree that would be necessary to cause its stock to appreciate at any meaningful rate. If we were at a track betting on a horse race, fixed-income investing would be like betting on horses merely making it around the track and finishing the race, as opposed to an equity investment that is more like betting on horses to excel, in other words, win, place, or show.

That is why we regard fixed-income investments as nonheroic in the sense that our performance expectations are modest compared to what investors expect and, indeed, require their equity investments to do to achieve success. Prime candidates for us to consider in populating our Income Factory, fixed-income securities are generally defined as those that provide periodic income payments at a dividend or interest rate that is known in advance by the investor, and which does not change. The most common examples of fixed-income investments are US Treasury and corporate bonds, corporate loans, preferred stock, bank certificates of deposit (CDs), fixed annuities, and defined benefit pension plans.

When considering candidates for our Income Factory, we have both *expanded* that definition in one sense, and *narrowed* it in another. We have narrowed it inasmuch as we are only considering fixed-income securities that pay us a high distribution yield, which we define as a yield equal to, or at least fairly close to, the equity return (i.e., 8% to 10%) that we defined earlier. So we limit ourselves to the high-yield end of the fixed-income spectrum, thus eliminating low-yielding securities like bank CDs, or US Treasury and investment grade corporate bonds, none of which pay more than about 4% or 5%, at the most.

However, we also have expanded the definition of fixed income to include a wider array of investments than just high-yield bonds and preferred stock, which are probably what most investors typically regard as high-yielding fixed-income investments. We include in our definition virtually any asset class that pays a high yield as a matter of course, whether it is technically a bond, a stock, a loan, or some other type of security. The key is that we look for asset classes where the cash distribution alone is high enough to provide us with the equity return we are seeking, and anything else—dividend growth, market price appreciation, special distributions—is icing on the cake but not our main reason for making that investment choice. Note that just because a high-yielding stock, bond, fund or other asset meets our definition of *fixed income* doesn't automatically mean we consider it a candidate for our Income Factory. That's just the starting point, after which we need to carry out due diligence as to its record, future prospects, and income potential. Some securities may not make the cut for our core list of Income Factory candidates, but are suitable candidates—in smaller dosages—for spicing up returns.

Our expanded list of high-yielding fixed income candidates includes:

- Leveraged loans, which is the term the credit markets use to describe large floating rate, senior secured corporate loans to non-investment grade companies (i.e., companies rated BB+ and below by the major rating agencies; BBB– and above is considered "investment grade")
- High-yield bonds, which are fixed rate bonds issued to the same cohort of non-investment grade companies as the loan category mentioned previously; the difference being that the bonds are unsecured and junior to the senior secured loans in priority of repayment in the event of default
- Preferred stocks
- Convertible securities
- Utilities, master limited partnerships (MLPs), business development companies (BDCs), most of which, while equities, emphasize high, stable, current cash distributions over growth
- Specialized vehicles, like asset-backed securities, especially collateralized loan obligations (CLOs) and other highly leveraged funds or exchange-traded funds and notes (ETFs and ETNs)
- Closed-end funds that hold equities, but use options strategies to essentially trade off future stock appreciation in return for higher and steadier current cash income

Some of these high-yield securities, like the specialized vehicles and highly leveraged ETFs and ETNs, carry substantial additional risk, which is why they pay abnormally high yields in the midteens and higher. We would only use these assets sparingly in our portfolio to spice up our returns as described previously. But our bread-and-butter high-yield assets, like loans, bonds, and other traditional fixed-income securities, generally carry no more risks than the typical stocks and bonds that most investors hold in their portfolios. However, they may not be the same risks, and to the extent they are less-familiar risks, they may actually feel riskier to many investors.

Asset classes labeled "high yield" have, unfortunately, developed a reputation for being riskier than I believe they actually are, for a number of reasons. First of all, the term *non-investment grade* itself has certain negative implications to begin with, its name suggesting that companies so described probably don't belong in someone's investment portfolio. Then the market goes a step further by automatically labeling the debt issued by non-investment grade companies as "high yield" and uses the market nickname "junk" to describe it. It is, therefore, no wonder many investors come to the conclusion that it must be very risky and unfit for their own portfolios.

As mentioned several chapters back in our comparison of lion tamers and tightrope walkers, it is normal for people to think that risks they are accustomed to taking are not as risky as those they are not so familiar with. In investing, we often view less familiar securities and asset classes as scarier than ones we are better acquainted with. That is why so many equity investors overestimate the degree of risk presented by high-yield credit investing compared to the risks in the stock portfolios that they already hold.

Risk and Return—Looking Under the Hood

Most investors were introduced to stocks early in their careers and have less exposure to bonds and other fixed-income securities, as well as to the risks they represent. So here we spend some time reviewing and comparing the risk/reward profiles presented by stocks, bonds, loans, and other fixed-income securities. Then we examine the returns available from these various asset classes and try to allocate the returns to the specific risks being taken. We may be surprised to discover that the returns we get or think we get do not always match up with the risks we are taking (i.e., with the bets we are making).

When we buy stock in a company we take equity risk. We become an owner of the company, paying the price that Mr. Market has determined a share of stock in that company is worth today. If the company pays a dividend, say 2% or 3%, then we collect that as an owner of the company. For us to make any more than that, the company has to grow—its sales, its earnings, its dividends, its overall net worth—so that it becomes worth more than it was when we bought it. If it does not grow, then there is no reason its value should ever be more than what we originally paid for it. In that case, we would earn our 2% or 3% per annum dividend and that would be it. When we finally sell the company, there is no reason to expect that we will get back any more than the original price we paid for it.

That's why an equity investment is essentially a growth bet. The company has to grow if the stock is going to be worth any more in the future than it was when we bought it. Not only that, if it doesn't grow and we collect our dividend and nothing more, then we probably won't be a very happy investor if all we earn is 3% or so. The only exception to that would be a company (like a high-yielding utility or one of the specialized companies we have mentioned, like MLPs or BDCs, that pay above-average distributions) whose dividends are high enough that many investors—like Income Factory investors—would buy the stock for the dividend alone and not really care if the stock price remained static.

The fixed-income market is simpler than the equity market in one sense. What you see is what you get in terms of cash flows. You typically get a fixed (or at least fairly static, with little or no anticipated growth) stream of payments for some foreseeable period of time (perhaps a fixed term or indefinite). So compared to an equity investment, whose value depends on future growth, which is rather unpredictable, your value with a fixed-income investment is fairly easy to project. You can apply various discount rates to the stream of assured or likely payments and come up with a discounted present value. Or you can merely project out the future stream of payments and forecast reinvestment and compounding rates based on that. The point is, by definition, it is fixed or largely so, and your projected return is not likely to vary much within a fairly narrow range of probable outcomes.

What is not always clear in either equity or fixed-income investments is exactly what risks we are taking with which securities. The three major investment risks that we take with stocks, bonds, and most other traditional securities are the following:

- Equity risk, just mentioned, is the risk of the company failing to grow its value, leaving us with a stock that is worth no more in the future than what we paid for it. Obviously, if the company loses value, because its earnings, business franchise, or both are depleted or destroyed, our stock's price can drop or it can become worthless.
- Credit risk, which is the risk that our issuer fails to pay its debts in general or fails to pay the specific debt that it owes to us. The risk of the company failing to pay all of it debts, and going bankrupt, is a risk not only creditors take, but also all equity owners as well, since if a company stiffs its creditors, it goes out of business and its stockholders generally get paid nothing as well.
- Interest rate risk, which is the risk that our bond or other fixed-income security may lose value in the future if interest rates rise and the future payment stream is then discounted at a higher market interest rate.

Every investment has at least one of these risks embedded in it, and most have two or more. So it is important that we understand which risks may or may not be incorporated in the particular asset classes and securities we select for our portfolio.

It is also important to try to understand how much of our anticipated yield or return is attributable to each of these risks. In other words, our investment involves a bet, or more likely several bets, and we should understand what we are betting on and how much we are compensated for taking each bet. As we will see later, our yield or anticipated return on the securities we consider purchasing for our Income Factory generally includes a number of separate components, each one—at least in theory—a return for one of the separate risks included in that particular investment.

For example, suppose a one-month US Treasury bill pays a yield of 2.25%, which it did, approximately, for much of 2019. This is an instrument with no credit risk, since the US government can issue all the dollars it wants or needs to, so there is no credit risk as long as it borrows in US dollars. Of course, that is not the case when a country has to issue debt in currencies it does not control, as Argentina's creditors, for example, understand very well. The US Treasury bill also carries virtually no interest-rate risk, since its term—one month— is so short that whatever interest-rate risk exists would be negligible. Again, this would not necessarily be the case in a hyperinflationary economy, like post–World War I Germany or current Venezuela, where short-term interest rates skyrocket along with prices on virtually a daily basis.

Because it carries essentially no credit risk or interest-rate risk, the short-term US Treasury bill rate is considered the risk-free rate. This risk-free rate—recently about 2.25%—is what the market charges for the inconvenience or opportunity cost of investors foregoing the use of their own money—that is, letting someone else use it even where there is no risk of not getting it back or of its losing value because it is locked into a below-market interest rate. As you add interest-rate risk, usually by extending the term to maturity, that rate should go up (emphasize the word *should* since we have seen anomalies lately). As you add credit risk the rate should also go up. Finally, as you add equity risk, the return should go up even further.

Table 10.1 summarizes how the various risks layer up in any debt or equity instrument, from the risk-free base, through the interest-rate risk, credit-risk, and equity-risk layers. In theory, each of these risk layers should have an appropriate layer of reward in the total yield of the

TABLE 10.1 Debt and Equity Markets Risk/Reward "Layer Cake"

	What Investor Is Being Compensated For	Examples
Risk Free	Payment merely for the use of investor's money, but with no or negligible interest rate, credit, equity, or uncertainty risk	1–3-month T-Bills, overnight fed funds
Interest Rate Risk	Risk of fixing the interest rate for a period of time; investor risks submarket return or capital loss if rates rise	Term Treasury or corporate bonds, mortgages
Credit Risk	Risk that issuer will fail to pay its bills, debts and other obligations, and/or otherwise fail to remain in business	Debt instruments (notes, bonds, loans, mortgages) and equities
Equity Risk	Entrepreneurial risk that issuer will fail to grow sales, earnings, and overall business, providing little or no return to owners	Equities, stock options

instrument, and an investor should not move from a no-risk or low-risk instrument to increasingly risky layers of risk without being sure they are paid marginally more for each additional element of risk.

We shall see whether reality matches the theory. As we have said repeatedly, our goal is to achieve higher returns without necessarily having to take the higher risks that are often associated with that level of return. A classic way to do this is to look for situations where the market doesn't seem to appreciate what the risks are (or are not) and misprices them accordingly; or as we have discussed earlier, where the market is paying us to take risks that we aren't necessarily concerned about or don't find particularly worrisome.

Stocks—What Are the Risks?

Everyone knows that stocks, by definition, carry equity risk. That's the risk that the company essentially stagnates, in terms of building its business franchise and increasing its earnings and, ultimately, its dividends to shareholders. What is not realized so universally is that stocks also take on the credit risk of the company as well. To use our previous analogy of a horse race, the equity investor needs their horse to win, place, or show, but if it doesn't first make it around the track (i.e., win the *credit* bet), it has no chance of winning, placing, or showing (i.e., winning the equity bet).

Creditors of the company, including its bondholders, the banks and other investors who hold its loans, and of course its trade creditors, all directly assume the risk that the company will default on its obligations and fail to pay what it owes to them. These groups represent the classic corporate creditors—bank lenders, bondholders, and trade creditors—and the securities they hold (bonds, loans, accounts payable) are what we generally think of as debt or fixed-income securities. Preferred stock, although it includes "stock" in its name, is often included in the fixed-income list as well, since it is actually more like a bond in that its dividend is generally fixed like the coupon on a bond and does not have the upside potential to increase over time that dividends paid to stockholders do. Preferred stock also has certain downside protections (its accumulated dividends usually must be paid in full before new common stock dividends can be paid, and it gets its principal repaid in a corporate liquidation before common stockholders collect a distribution).

In summary, we expect investors in bonds, loans, preferred stock, and other holders of corporate debt and trade claims to regard themselves as creditors and the risk they are taking as credit risk. But it comes as a shock to many stockholders when we point out to them that, besides the equity and therefore the entrepreneurial risk they are taking, they are also assuming the credit risk of the company just as much as any creditor. Not only that, but they are taking *more* credit risk as an equity owner than they would if they were merely an ordinary lender, bondholder, or trade creditor.

That's because if a company defaults on its debt and fails to pay it, eventually it ends up in bankruptcy, goes out of business, and is liquidated. When that happens, the creditors get paid first with whatever assets are available and if there is anything left afterward, the equity owners get it. Sometimes, in complex bankruptcies, the various debt holders reach a compromise agreement with the equity owners, where the creditors share a portion of what they are entitled to receive with the stockholders to get them to go along peacefully and avoid a complex court battle. But in general, the equity gets very little or nothing compared to the direct creditors. In short, the stockholders are taking every bit as much credit risk as any debt holder further ahead of them in the capital structure, and in the event of what bankers call a credit event, like a default and eventual liquidation, the equity generally takes the largest loss.

Once we realize that the stockholders are taking both the entrepreneurial (equity) risk plus the credit risk of the company, then we have to ask ourselves, as stockholders, whether we are being adequately compensated for taking both risks. Obviously, it is hard to generalize about what should be the proper financial upside incentive for taking the equity risk of any particular company. Some firms have highly risky business models with lots of competition, easy entry for competitors, substantial technical and operational challenges, and other perils. Others may have highly risky financial models with substantial amounts of debt versus equity, lots of short-term obligations that need to be rolled over frequently, or unpredictable cash flows. By comparison, some companies have business models, financial models, or both that are more conservative. The combination of all these factors makes particular businesses more or less risky, and each equity investor must decide whether the earnings growth potential, current dividend and dividend growth prospects, and ultimate price appreciation expectations for a particular company are sufficient to justify the risk of owning its stock.

Doing that is a tough job, which is why investors like me leave it to professional analysts and fund managers to do the fundamental company-by-company analysis and create diversified funds that we then consider for inclusion in our portfolios. But there is one thing we do know for sure that should apply to any decision about whether to pay a certain price for a company's stock. Whatever your anticipated return on buying a company's stock is, it had better be *greater* than what you can get paid if you merely bought the company's debt. As a stockholder, you are taking all the risks the creditors take of the company going bust, plus you have the added disadvantage of being last in line if that happens. So anyone would be foolish to buy any company's stock and take all those risks without being confident the stock's total return will be greater than the interest rate paid to someone who merely purchased the company's debt.

As we shall see in our next chapter, where we discuss in more detail the risks, rewards, and yields on a variety of credit instruments, in most instances the naked yield on debt instruments is not as great as the anticipated return on stocks. Since our Income Factory goal is to achieve an equivalent equity yield by investing in nonequity fixed-income securities, that means we have a hurdle to overcome to boost the yield on our fixed-income investments to reach that equity return level. Hence our interest in closed-end funds and other specialized security types to help us make up that difference.

One irony worth mentioning is that many conventional equity investors insist they would never buy high-yield bonds because they are supposedly so risky. High-yield bonds (also sometimes called junk bonds) are merely bonds issued by non-investment grade companies, which means the companies are rated BB+ and below. That includes more than half of all companies, so most of the companies whose stocks are labeled "mid-cap" and "small cap" are, in fact, non-investment grade companies. A great many of the same investors who insist so vehemently they would never buy junk bonds have portfolios chock-full of stock from the same cohort of companies, in their mid-cap and small-cap equity portfolios. But, of course, the equity of those companies is far riskier, because it is further down the capital structure and thus junior to the very junk bonds that they insist they would never own. Go figure.

Bonds, Interest Rates, and Credit Risk

In the last chapter we introduced our Income Factory's expansive definition of *fixed income* as including a number of asset classes, all of which have in common the idea of a steady cash flow high enough to meet our equity return target without having to grow earnings or dividends. We also introduced the idea that our fixed income yields can be subdivided into discrete layers of return covering (1) the risk-free rate for merely making our money available to a third party, (2) interest rate risk, (3) credit risk, and in some cases, (4) equity risk. We further noted that equity risk incorporates credit risk within it, since a business that stiffs its creditors is also worthless to its stockholders.

In this chapter we drill down further into some traditional fixed-income asset classes to see which risks investors are taking and how they are being compensated for it. For example, we describe how most of the yield on Treasury bonds and investment grade corporate bonds represents the risk-free compensation for letting third parties use our money, along with payment for the embedded interest rate bet, with minimal credit risk or compensation for taking it.

By contrast, high-yield corporate bonds have shorter terms and therefore, much less interest-rate risk than Treasury bonds and investment-grade corporate bonds, so they represent a real credit bet as opposed to an interest-rate bet, and investors get paid for taking it.

* * *

Traditional Bonds— Interest-Rate Risk Versus Credit Risk

Since fixed income, bonds, and credit are all important elements of our Income Factory strategy, it is worth spending some time discussing the debt market in general, which sectors of it we want to participate in, and why.

Table 11.1 lists the most common types of debt instruments: (1) short-term US Treasury bills and Fed funds with maturities ranging from overnight to a couple months and coupons recently just slightly above 2%, (2) Treasury bonds with fixed interest rates and maturities of typically 10 to 30 years out, and coupon rates recently in the range of 2.25% to 2.5%, (3) investment grade corporate bonds with fixed rates, again with maturities typically of 10 years or more and recent coupon rates in the 3.5% to 4.5% range depending on credit ratings, and (4) high-yield corporate, fixed-rate bonds to non-investment grade companies, with shorter terms typically in the 5-to-10-year range and yields of 6% to 10% and higher, depending on credit ratings and deal structure. Please note that Table 11.1 is labeled "Illustrative" bond market rates, since rates vary considerably over time, especially recently as the Federal Reserve has had to cope with enormous economic and geopolitical uncertainties in formulating its interest rate policy.

As noted back in Table 10.1 in the last chapter, fixed-income investors are paid for a variety of things: (1) the inconvenience and opportunity cost associated with letting someone else have the use of

TABLE 11.1 Most Common Types of Debt Instruments

Illustrative Bond Market Rates		Spread Over Risk-Free Rate
US T-Bills/Fed Funds	2.25%	NA
US Treasury—10 Year	2.25%	0.00%
US Treasury—30 Year	2.50%	0.25%
AAA Corp	3.50%	1.25%
BBB Corp	4.50%	2.25%
BB Corp	6.00%	3.75%
B Corp	7.50%	5.25%
CCC Corp	10.00%	7.75%

their money, (2) the risk that the money won't be worth as much in purchasing power when they get it back, (3) the related risk that interest rates will have risen and they will have earned a submarket rate during the period of the investment (or a capital loss if they decide to sell the bond before maturity and receive a discounted price because its coupon rate is below the current market rate), and (4) the credit risk of the issuer defaulting and failing to pay interest or principal. All four of these risks are intensified and exacerbated through the passage of time and the uncertainty associated with that. So we expect to see some sort of "uncertainty premium" tacked onto the yield as maturities extend further and further out, but as we shall see, that is not always the case.

What jumps out at us as we look at Table 11.1 is *how little* investors have gotten paid recently for taking the additional interest rate and uncertainty risk of committing their money for 10 years or even 30 years. Note that the risk-free rate you get paid for lending your money to the government for a mere month or so has been about 2.25% (including the rate banks get paid for lending each other the overnight deposits they have at the Federal Reserve itself). That's what you would have earned on a portfolio of short-term Treasury bills, or alternatively, on a Vanguard Federal Money Market Fund, which holds short-term government securities. We call it risk-free because the government can print all the dollars it wants, so there is no risk of not being paid back. And there is little risk of an interest rate rise hurting an investment that is only for a month or so.

But there is real interest-rate risk when you go out from two or three months to 10 years or 30 years, and an additional 0.1% for 10 years (lately it has even been zero at times) or 0.25% for 30 years is not much compensation. Historically the yield on 30-year Treasury bonds has been about 3% higher than the yield on short-term Treasury bills. Most market observers believe the recent flatness in the yield curve is an anomaly that understates the real long-term interest rate risk. It may just be a temporary phenomenon, a sign of possible near-term weakness in the economy, in which case the natural difference between short-term and long-term rates eventually will reassert itself. That means we have to be somewhat careful in assuming how a US Treasury bond coupon is split between the risk-free portion and the part that compensates for the interest rate bet, as it will vary periodically as the slope of the yield curve changes.

Although there may be no real credit risk on US government bonds, that is not to say there is no risk, especially with the long-dated ones. While we can be confident the US Treasury will pay investors the dollar amount of the bond principal, what those dollars are worth in the future depends on future rates of inflation, and that is a critical factor in projecting future interest rates and evaluating the interest-rate risk. In the higher-inflation scenario, interest rates would invariably rise along with inflation. And if you wanted to get your money back before maturity, you would have to sell the bond at a lower price, one determined by discounting its future cash flows at the higher interest rate levels.

Alternatively, you could grit your teeth and just accept the bond's coupon until the end of the 10-year (or 30-year) term. In that case you would, at maturity, receive the full face value of the bond so you would not suffer any loss of principal. But you would have had to accept a below-market level of interest for the remaining life of the bond from whatever point the rise in interest rates occurred. One way or another you lose if interest rates rise at any point in the life of the bond.

Even if interest rates never rise during the 10 to 30 years that you own the bond, you are still stuck with a substandard 3% earnings rate (or less) for a decade or longer. So your real cost for hedging or balancing your portfolio with bonds is the loss of the income you would have received had you been fully invested in higher-yielding assets. Your opportunity cost in that case is the difference between whatever yield you were earning (or could have been earning) on the rest of your portfolio, say 8% or 10%, and the 3% or so you earned on your "safe" Treasury bonds.

Corporate Bonds and Credit Risk

Suppose instead of buying the Treasury bonds, you bought a corporate bond issued by a triple-A rated company. Now you would be getting a coupon in the range of 3.5%, perhaps 1.25% higher than the 10-year Treasury bond. But you have also added credit risk to your bet, in addition to the interest-rate risk, and you are receiving only an additional 1.25% for taking that risk. Admittedly, triple-A companies rarely default, as Table 11.2 (next page) shows, but on the rare occasions they do, investors tend to lose most of their principal since (1) the bonds are unsecured (triple-A borrowers are virtually never asked to provide collateral, so when they do default, creditors are essentially naked), and (2) triple-A companies are always well-established icons in the business world, so when one actually defaults, it usually involves either a scandal of some sort or a long, prolonged death that leaves little for unsecured creditors to salvage.

If we move down into the triple-B rated corporate bond arena, we face the same question of whether we are being compensated adequately for the additional credit risk we are now taking on. Again we have the same underlying interest-rate risk and opportunity cost that we had with the Treasury bond. But now we have a triple-B corporate credit risk as opposed to the triple-A risk in our previous example.

Compared to bonds of triple-A rated credits paying us 3.5%, or 1.25% above 10-year Treasury bonds, triple-B rated bonds would probably pay about 4.5%. That's an additional 1% above Treasury bonds, for a total of 2.25% that we are being paid to take credit risk, over and above the risk-free opportunity cost and interest-rate risk already embedded in the 10-year Treasury bond rate of 2.25%.

TABLE 11.2 Corporate Default Rates over Time

Rating Category	Cumulative Default Rate After 5 Years	Cumulative Default Rate Annualized	Increased Incidence of Default Between Rating Categories	
AAA/A	0.4%	0.08%	—	
BBB	1.6%	0.33%	4.2	Times AAA/A Rate
BB	6.8%	1.40%	4.1	Times BBB Rate
B	17.0%	3.50%	2.6	Times BB Rate
CCC/C	46.0%	9.20%	2.7	Times B Rate

Data Source: Standard & Poor's *Default, Transition & Recovery: 2018 Annual Global Corporate Default and Rating Transition Study*

Obviously, 4.5% is a better return than what we were being paid to hold either a Treasury bond or a triple-A corporate. And it comes close to matching the current dividend income we would be receiving from the portfolio of dividend growth investing (DGI) stocks that we might have chosen to include in our Income Factory Light. But unlike those stocks, which we expect to pay us 5% in cash *plus* grow their dividends and stock prices over time, with the bonds the coupon interest is all we will ever get. In other words, it's called "fixed income" for a reason. No future growth, unless interest rates should unexpectedly move down rather than up over the next decade or so. That seems pretty unlikely (except for short-term movements) at this point in an interest rate cycle that has seen interest rates fall over a 35-year period and are still at their lowest point since the 1950s. In other words, this does not seem like a time to be betting on a long-term downward shift in interest rates, which is what a purchase of Treasury or investment grade corporate bonds represents.

Down the Credit Rating Scale:
Different Risk, More Return

Unlike triple-A bonds, with triple-B bonds there is a real risk of default and loss. According to historical default statistics, a triple-B credit is about four times as likely to default as any bond with an "A" in its rating, single-A, double-A, or triple-A. So when you buy a triple-B bond you are getting at least four times the credit risk as a triple-A, but less than twice the compensation (2.25% versus 1.25%, above the risk-free rate) for taking that credit risk.

As you move down the rating scale even further, the apparent returns for taking credit risk do not appear, on the surface, to compensate investors for the additional risk. Double-B credits are about four times as likely to default as triple-Bs, and yet the extra spread over Treasury yields for moving from triple-Bs to double-Bs has recently only been about 1.5%. Moving from double-B credits down to single-Bs has netted investors only a further 1.5% spread, despite single-Bs being over twice as likely to default, as measured by historical default statistics.

To summarize, longer-term Treasury bond investors get paid very little for taking the enormous additional interest rate risk of going out 10 to 30 years, while investment grade corporate bond investors don't get much more for taking both interest-rate risk and credit risk. The apparent under-compensation continues as you move further down the credit spectrum to single-B-rated issuers, where the coupon increases to about 7.5% or more, depending on the credit and the deal structure. The "or more" is important to emphasize here, as prices widen out considerably as you move deeper into lower investment grade territory and deals that bankers and underwriters consider particularly risky can carry coupons far higher than the category averages.

But even assuming an average rate of 7.5%, or over 5% above Treasury bond coupons, a single-B investor may still appear to be receiving only minimal additional compensation (compared to triple-A, triple-B, and double-B borrowers) for an asset class that has historically defaulted at least twice as often as double-B issuers, and about eight or nine times as often as triple-Bs. So the question jumps out at us: Are high-yield bond investors being paid sufficiently for the additional credit risk they are taking, or are they irrationally accepting more credit risk for relatively less reward as they move down the credit spectrum? Or is something else going on? The answer, as is so often the case when something looks out of kilter, is "Yes, there is something else going on."

High-Yield Credit, with the Emphasis on Credit

The main difference between high-yield credit, both loans and bonds, and traditional higher-grade debt (Treasury bonds and investment grade bonds) is the amount of interest rate risk that is taken, or in the case of most high-yield debt, *not taken*, by the investors in each asset class. Treasury bonds and most investment grade bonds have fixed interest rates and maturities that run out 10 years and longer (up to 30 years for Treasuries and some of the highest rated corporates, and out past 20 years for many other investment grade corporates). That means it is totally appropriate that investors allocate 2.5% or 3% or even more just for the interest rate and overall uncertainty risk that is embedded in these bonds, before even thinking about being compensated for the credit risk that they have undertaken.

High-yield bonds, by contrast, are shorter term, so even though they have fixed interest rates, they tend to mature and be replaced every 5 or 6 years, rather than every 10-, 15-, or 20-plus years like Treasury bonds and investment grade corporates. If we invest in diversified pools of high-yield bonds, like the funds we hold in our Income Factories, then about 20% or so of our portfolio is replaced and repriced in the first year after any interest rate increase, with virtually the entire portfolio repriced to the higher rate level within four or five years.

That means high-yield investors do not have to set aside the 2.5% or 3% or whatever rate at which Mr. Market decides to price the interest rate bet of a long-term Treasury bond and deduct it from the return they receive for taking credit risk. Assuming (and it varies widely from portfolio to portfolio) that our shorter-term high-yield portfolios might have only a quarter or one-third or even less the interest rate risk of typical Treasury/investment grade portfolios, we can probably regard the embedded cost of the interest rate bet in our high-yield portfolios as more like 0.5% to 1% rather than the 2.5% or higher interest rate bet cost implied by Treasury bond pricing.

We should note that our analysis here is, admittedly, intuitive more than scientific. That is because we can seldom determine for sure how much additional yield or return the market requires or should require to compensate for certain risks. It seems obvious to many of us that interest rate movements and macro-economic trends in general are easier to project and plan for just a few years into the future than they are 10, 20, or 30 years out. But how much more should we be paid for taking the risk 10 years out versus 5 years out, or 20 years out versus 10 years out? How do we evaluate this "unknowability" factor, or how much investors should be compensated for taking it?

Is it a purely *linear* increase in risk, or does the amount of uncertainty and anxiety and all the other unpleasant tangible and intangible aspects of interest rate risk over time increase at an *exponential* rate as we project further into a distant and increasingly murky future? Personally I think the risk grows exponentially as you move further out, and in my own evaluation, I have weighted it accordingly. That's why I believe there is relatively little interest-rate risk in a five-year high-yield portfolio that reprices relatively quickly and where the time period in which any adverse interest rate changes are likely to occur is reasonably foreseeable. Compare that to long-term fixed rate bonds that may carry less credit risk but far more interest rate risk, especially many years or even decades into the future.

When you adjust for the interest rate bet differential, the pure credit risk compensation for high-yield bonds appears more rational. The single-B corporate that pays a coupon of 7.5% or higher, with virtually all of it available to compensate for credit risk, now compares more favorably with a triple-A corporate earning only 1.25% for credit risk, or a triple-B corporate that earns 2.5%. The double-B corporate's

6% return also looks pretty attractive, once we understand that, like the single-Bs, very little of it needs to be allocated to covering interest rate risk. This view is supported by the fact that historical data shows high-yield bond returns have actually been negatively correlated with returns on Treasury and investment grade bonds. In other words, the interest rate moves that so affect Treasury bonds and investment grade corporates have much less effect on high-yield bonds. (They have even less impact—virtually none—on loans to high-yield corporate borrowers, whose coupons are readjusted every one to three months.)

Bottom Line: Connecting the Dots

The two main points of Chapters 10 and 11 have been that:

- Credit risk is embedded in the risk that traditional equity investors take, and therefore rational investors should not buy stock and take the additional risk of being further down the capital structure, unless the anticipated upside reward for stock ownership is clearly greater than the interest rate you would earn as a debt holder.
- When you strip out the overall interest rate bet component of the coupon paid to bondholders (Treasury, investment grade corporates, and high-yield corporates), it appears obvious that the high-yield sector actually gets paid substantially more for taking credit risk, compared to the other two sectors (Treasury and investment grade corporate).

Let's put these two ideas together and see what the implications are. We can get paid 6% or 7% and higher (as we see in later chapters) for taking only credit risk by buying a portfolio of high-yielding, fixed-income securities. Investors in stock, if they are smart enough to buy and hold and resist the urge to do something foolish when market pressures increase, typically make about 8% to 10% over the long term. That means equity investors are being paid an extra 3% or so for taking all the additional equity risks that creditors don't have to worry about.

Readers obviously know by now that an extra 3%, compounded over decades, makes a huge difference in total return and—expressing it in Income Factory terms—in the size of the income stream that represents the output of the factory. Our goal, in structuring our Income Factory, is to figure out how to get that debt/equity differential of 3% down to zero so we can earn the full equity return of 8% to 10% completely (or almost completely) through fixed-income securities, thus avoiding equity risks without sacrificing equity-type returns. In the next two chapters, we take an even deeper dive into certain fixed-income and other asset classes to see how we can use them to close that 3% gap.

Senior Loans (High-Yield Bonds with Benefits)

In the last two chapters we discussed the role of fixed income, especially debt instruments, in our Income Factory strategy. We noted that traditional high-quality bonds, like Treasury and investment grade corporate bonds, pay investors more for taking interest-rate risk than for taking credit risk; and they don't pay all that much for either one.

High-yield corporate bonds, on the other hand, have shorter terms and therefore less interest-rate risk. Of course, as non-investment grade bonds they also have lower credit ratings and greater risk of default, which justifies their higher yields ranging from 6% to low double digits, depending on credit quality. We noted our long-term equity-return target range is 8% to 10% and that we need to be creative if we want to reach that using fixed-income-type investments.

In this chapter we begin to explore how to do that, especially using secured corporate loans that sit at the top of an issuer's balance sheet (above the bonds and equity), get paid first in the event of trouble, and offer unique opportunities to income investors. Understanding how they do that requires a deeper look into the credit world, in particular, a discussion of how credit loss involves a two-dimensional analysis, one that considers both the risk of default and the expected loss and recovery in the event of default. For investors in high-yield credit, the plot thickens.

* * *

Loans—the Top of the Capital Structure

Corporate loans are a unique subset of the high-yield debt market. *High yield*, or the less complimentary "junk" label, refers to debt issued by non-investment grade corporations. "Investment grade" means any credit rating from AAA to BBB–, so non-investment grade includes any rating below that, from BB+ down to D. In practice, we seldom see a new issue rated lower than CCC, a rating that suggests the issuer has little margin of safety or room for maneuver if its business plan does not work out as expected. Ratings below that (CC, C, or D) all mean the rating agency believes default is almost a certainty at some point in the future, or in the case of D, has already occurred.

The cohort of companies that are included in the so-called junk or non-investment grade category is huge, and includes many large familiar firms. In fact, most of the mid-cap and small-cap companies whose stock so many investors happily hold in their portfolios (either individually or through mutual funds) are rated non-investment grade, or would be if they were to obtain credit ratings. Ironically, many of those same investors, if queried, would probably tell us they consider high-yield *debt* to be junk that is too risky for them to own, without realizing they hold the *stock* of the same cohort of companies in their equity portfolios. They would be surprised to learn that stock is a lot riskier than the debt of the companies they insist they would never buy, since equity ranks at the bottom of the capital structure and gets paid last (i.e., after the debt) if the company gets into financial trouble.

Default Versus Loss

If we want to understand credit and how to invest in it, we should start with the distinction between default and loss. Default means failure to pay on time. If a debtor fails to make an interest, principal, rent, trade credit, or other payment when it is due, that is a default. Defaults, if not rectified, can lead to business failure, bankruptcy, liquidation, or any combination of these.

From a credit investor's standpoint, default is just the first step in the process that eventually results in a credit loss to the investor's portfolio. A credit loss is the difference between how much a creditor recovers in the bankruptcy or liquidation process, and how much they were actually owed. If a debtor defaults and owes you $1 million and you eventually recover $750,000, then your loss is the difference, or $250,000.

How much a creditor (i.e., bondholder, bank lender) recovers when a borrower (i.e., bond or note issuer) defaults depends on several factors:

- Is the creditor secured or unsecured? Do they have mortgages or liens on specific assets of the borrower that can be sold and the proceeds used to repay them?
- Where is their debt on the borrower's balance sheet in relation to other debt claims? Are they senior to other creditors in terms of having first dibs on the borrower's assets, or are they "junior" or "subordinated" and don't get paid until after more senior creditors are repaid?
- What sort of company is the borrower and what sort of assets do they have? Do they have "hard" assets that are readily marketable, or are their assets more intangible or less likely to have or retain value in a bankruptcy or liquidation?

The dirty little secret about credit ratings—AAA through D—is that the traditional ratings that have been in use for the past century *only* address the likelihood of default, and except in very rare instances, say nothing about the prospects for recovery or loss after default. This worked fine for decades because almost all issuers' public debt was single-class debt, which meant that all the notes or bonds of a single issuer would rank *pari passu*—that is, equally—in the event of default and bankruptcy. That meant no particular class of bond or note from each borrower would have an advantage over other creditors, so there was little reason to differentiate among them. Equally important was the general attitude of investors whose primary goal was to avoid default and who had little interest in analyzing what defaulted bonds would be worth post-default. Nor did most public debt holders (pension funds, mutual funds, insurance companies, etc.) have much interest in getting involved in the "workout process," the grubbier side of banking and credit investing where you had to chase down, foreclose, or otherwise liquidate your collateral, if you were lucky enough to have any, or negotiate with other creditors over how to divide up the carcass of your now defunct borrower.

So for all these reasons, and mostly because credit ratings had "always been done that way" and there was no particular incentive to change it, the public debt market continued to use one-dimensional, default-only ratings until the mid-1990s.

Enter Bank Loans, the "Asset Class"

The impetus for change began when corporate bank loans (i.e., the loans commercial banks make to corporations) started to become a separate investment "asset class" in the late 1980s and early 1990s. Banks had been lending to companies for centuries, but as long as the banks kept the loans on their own books and did their own credit analysis, there was no need for a rating to tell other investors how good (or bad) the credit risk was. The banks prided themselves on the quality of the credit analysis they did on their clients and even considered it a competitive advantage *not* to have the rest of the world know exactly how they regarded the credit of their own clients. Once another bank understood your client's credit as well as you did, it was just a matter of time before they were knocking on the client's door and trying to take the business away from you.

For many generations, big banks had been "participating" pieces of their large commercial loans to smaller "correspondent" banks. The correspondent banks, in theory, did their own credit analysis on the loan being participated to them. In practice, they often relied heavily on the reputation and expertise of the bank that initiated the deal and maintained the relationship with the borrower. One way or the other, the credit was kept "in the family," so to speak, and no credit ratings were required.

But loans became larger and their maturities longer, especially as commercial bankers learned that they could compete with the more highly paid investment bankers down the street by offering term loans instead of high-yield bonds to finance mergers, acquisitions, and other big ticket transactions. This meant expanding the potential investor base for loans beyond just other commercial banks to the wider world of pensions, mutual funds, insurance companies, endowments, and other institutional investors.

But if bankers wanted to start underwriting and distributing their loans to large institutional investors, those loans would need to have credit ratings, just like traditional bonds. This presented a problem to bankers, who for years had been lending to lower-rated companies (i.e., borrowers with higher propensities to default) by structuring the loans in ways that improved their recovery prospects even if the borrower defaulted. Those bankers knew from experience that their loans to lower-rated or unrated borrowers, secured by collateral and other structural features, were typically better credits than many of the unsecured bonds and notes currently being issued by higher-rated companies. But if the only ratings available at that time were traditional default ratings that failed to capture the added dimension of collateral and post-default recovery enhancement, then getting a rating would be counterproductive. All it would do was emphasize the borrowers' relatively high risk of default without showing how well protected the loans were in the event such a default occurred.

This challenge was remedied in the mid-1990s when some of the major rating agencies introduced recovery ratings to their lineup of analytical services. This allowed well-secured loans to more highly default-prone borrowers to be analyzed and rated on a more equal footing with bonds and notes issued by more highly rated companies, which were less likely to default (but if they did, would cost their creditors more in ultimate losses due to the lack of collateral security or other protections). The embrace of a two-dimensional analysis of debt, one that considers both the recovery expectation as well as the likelihood of default, seems pretty obvious now. But it was a radical departure in the financial industry when first introduced. For an up-close-and-personal account of how it happened, and an insight into how serendipitous and accidental financial innovation can be, see Appendix, "Financial Innovation: A Case Study," which chronicles the "invention" of bank loan ratings.

Two-Dimensional Credit Modeling

One reason the banking and investment community ended up welcoming the new two-dimensional approach to rating debt was that it mirrored the direction in which credit risk analysis was being done internally by both commercial banks and investors. To create loan loss reserves (in a bank) or to project credit losses (in an investment portfolio) the bankers or investors had to first project what percentage of their loans or bonds would default. Then they went the next step and tried to estimate what percentage of the defaulted principal would actually be repaid and, even more relevant to their bottom line, what percentage would be lost.

For example, Case 1 in Table 12.1 shows a conservative bond portfolio that only holds bonds or notes issued by investment grade issuers, with a very low expectation of default across the portfolio (0.33% in our example). Of course, because they are investment grade, they will almost certainly be unsecured, which means the expected recovery will be lower, and the expected loss will be higher (typically 50% for unsecured bonds) than for bonds or loans secured by collateral (losses typically only 25%). But even with the higher projected losses on the deals that default, the overall portfolio loss (i.e., the default rate times the rate of loss for issues that do default) is still quite low, at only 0.17%, because of the low default rate.

TABLE 12.1 Calculating Credit Losses: Case 1
Investment Grade Bond—BBB Rating—Unsecured

Average Annual Default Rate (% of Portfolio That Defaults)	Expected Loss if Issuer Defaults	Portfolio Loss (0.33% × 50%)
0.33%	50%	0.17%

Case 2 shows a more aggressive portfolio that is invested in high-yield, B-rated bonds. These will have a much higher likely rate of default, and since they are bonds they are still unsecured and likely to recover the same relatively modest amount (50%) that we saw with the unsecured investment grade bonds. In the example in Table 12.2, we see the result: the relatively high likely default rate of 3.5% combined with the higher loss expectation (50%) results in a projected portfolio loss rate of 1.75%.

TABLE 12.2 Calculating Credit Losses: Case 2
High-Yield Bond—B Rating—Unsecured

Average Annual Default Rate (% of Portfolio That Defaults)	Expected Loss If Issuer Defaults	Portfolio Loss (3.5% × 50%)
3.5%	50%	1.75%

Which of those two bond portfolios is a better investment? That will depend on several factors, the most important of which is what sort of a yield we are being offered to take the two risks. In the last chapter (Table 11.1) we noted that triple-B bond investors were collecting yields of about 4.5% recently, although we also noted that about half of that was compensation for taking the interest-rate risk and the uncertainty of committing to a term of 10 years or longer. That means the triple-B investor is really only being paid a net amount of about 2% to 2.5% for taking credit risk. The single-B bond investor is probably being paid in the range of 7.5% or possibly more, with most of that allocated to compensating them for credit risk, given that the maturities of most high-yield bonds are typically less than 10 years. Bottom line? Many investors, myself included, believe the additional compensation makes it worth taking the high-yield risk, especially if we can improve the odds by (1) choosing funds managed by experienced credit professionals, and (2) using closed-end funds that can use cheap leverage and be bought at discounts, both of which add additional spread to our yields.

Adding corporate loans to the mix makes the choices credit investors have even more interesting. Note that the third example shown in Table 12.3 involves a loan to a single-B borrower, just like the high-yield bond just mentioned. But because it is a senior, secured loan, it ranks above the unsecured bond and has first claim on most or all of the borrower's assets. Historically, secured corporate loans that default have recovered about 75% or more of their outstanding principal, which means, of course, that their losses have been 100% minus 75%, or 25%. Unsecured debt, by comparison, has historically recovered only 50% of its principal when it defaults, which means its average losses have been 50%, which is twice the average loss of loans. That means a portfolio of senior secured loans will likely have only about one-half the credit losses of a portfolio of high-yield bonds to the same cohort of non-investment grade companies. Put another way, high-yield bonds are twice as risky as loans to high-yield companies.

TABLE 12.3 Calculating Credit Losses: Case 3

Corporate Loan—B Rating—Secured

Average Annual Default Rate (% of Portfolio That Defaults)	Expected Loss If Issuer Defaults	Portfolio Loss (3.5% × 25%)
3.5%	25%	0.875%

But the story gets even better when you consider that corporate loans are also floating rate, with a typical loan based on the one- or three-month London InterBank Offered Rate (LIBOR)* plus a spread ranging from 3.5% to 5% or higher depending on the credit rating. With short-term LIBOR in the 2.5% range recently, that means an investor in loans can collect 6% or more, with only half the credit risk and none of the interest-rate risk of bonds. It is because of this that many credit professionals and portfolio managers regard corporate loans as somewhere on the risk/reward spectrum between money market funds and corporate bonds. (See Figure 12.1.)

FIGURE 12.1 Risk/Reward Spectrum

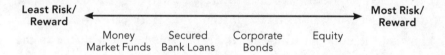

Money market funds have negligible credit risk and interest rate risk. Corporate bonds, as we have seen, have either lots of credit risk and minimal interest rate risk (if they are high-yield corporates), or minimal credit risk and lots of interest-rate risk (investment grade corporates). Loans fit in the middle between bonds and money market funds. They are obviously nowhere near as safe an investment as money market funds. But loans carry much higher coupons, and with their collateral and floating rates they are arguably a safer and better compensated bet than corporate bonds, especially investment grade ones.

Souping up Loan Returns

In recent decades, senior secured, floating-rate loans have proven themselves as a stable, steady-Eddie asset class capable of delivering an

---

* The global banking industry has plans to phase out LIBOR in 2021 and replace it with alternative benchmarks for various currencies. For the US dollar, it is expected to be replaced by the Secured Overnight Financing Rate (SOFR).

average total return of about 5%, with no interest rate risk and fairly predictable and controllable credit risk. That makes them a great balancer and diversifier in many portfolios, playing the role that investors have often looked to bonds to play, but without the interest-rate risk.

Attractive as that might be, 5% doesn't excite an institutional investor seeking an equity return of 10% or so. But we have seen earlier that loans, in a closed-end fund with some cheap institutional leverage and occasionally available at discounted prices, can generate distribution yields around 8%, which is the bottom end of our equity return target range. In addition, since loans sit at the top of the capital structure and take much less risk than equity, which resides at the very bottom, they are obviously much safer.

That led financial engineers to decide there ought to be a way to leverage such a well-secured, floating rate asset class—loans—and generate the same return as an unleveraged investment in the riskier asset class—equity. And since credit defaults and losses have proven over time to be more predictable than ups and downs in the equity market, perhaps the leveraged loan vehicle would generate that equity return with less volatility.

That was the theory behind the creation of collateralized loan obligations (CLOs). Now, three decades later, the CLO asset class has proven itself by its strong performance through the great recession/crash of 2008, as well as the periods before and since. It has also moved from being strictly an institutional investor product to now being available, through a number of funds, to the retail investment community, including Income Factory investors.

Although nothing is certain (especially about the future, to paraphrase Yogi Berra), CLOs have provided consistent rates of return to equity investors in the low teens and higher for several decades. I regard them as one of the best investments available to us if we want to spice up our Income Factory and add that extra 1% or so to our overall portfolio return. In our next chapter we describe how CLOs are designed and constructed, and discuss some of their obvious attractions, as well as the issues and challenges investors like us may have in understanding them and being comfortable with them in our portfolios.

Virtual Banks (aka "CLOs")

Many years ago there was an adage about bankers that they lived and worked according to the 3-6-3 rule. They paid their customers 3% on their deposits, loaned the money out at 6%, and were on the golf course by 3:00 P.M. Nice work if you could get it.

Mythical and overly simplistic as that maxim may be, there is a germ of truth in it and anyone who truly gets it will understand immediately how collateralized loan obligations (CLOs) work. For those who don't, we have this chapter.

The key to understanding CLOs is to realize that they are virtual banks. When you buy the equity in a CLO, it is like buying the stock of a bank, where the bank/CLO acquires a portfolio of loans that pay a rate (perhaps 7% or so) using funds that include its own capital (i.e., our money, as investors), plus money the bank/CLO borrows from a lot of other investors, at rates designed to average out to 4% or thereabouts.

The bigger the spread between what the CLO (or bank) pays its creditors (or depositors) and what it charges its own borrowing customers, and the more money it can borrow (or deposits it can attract) at that lower rate and relend at the higher rate, the more profit the CLO (or bank) will make—at least in theory.

Whether it is a bank or a CLO, the owners at the bottom of the balance sheet get all the excess spread between the 7% interest received and the 4% interest paid out. They also take all the losses from borrowers who fail to pay. That's where it gets interesting.

*   *   *

CLOs—Capital Structure Designed for Income

If ever there were an asset class that seems like it was designed for an Income Factory, it would be collateralized loan obligations. The assets that are the "raw material" from which CLOs are constructed are senior, secured floating-rate term loans to non-investment grade corporations. These loans are secured by collateral and have a long, well-documented history of protecting creditors even when they default, with recoveries averaging in the 75% to 80% range. (To be conservative, we will use 75% recovery assumptions in our examples that follow.) As a result, loans have less than half the credit losses of high-yield bonds (whose recovery rates are less than 50%) and carry no interest rate risk because their coupons are reset every one to three months at a spread above the London InterBank Offered Rate (LIBOR).

An ordinary investment in a portfolio of high-yield corporate loans (also known as leveraged loans) would generate coupon income of about 7%, depending on the credit ratings of the borrowers in the portfolio. If you want to earn more than that, the typical way investors do it is to leverage their investment by borrowing additional money at a lower rate, say 4%, and investing in more loans at 7%. Of course, you won't make as much net income on that second batch of loans as you do on the first batch because you used your own money on the first batch and don't have to share the income with anyone, while the first 4% of income received on the second batch is owed to the lenders who provided you with the additional funds.

To summarize, your naked investment in the loans, using just your own capital and no leverage, earned you a coupon of 7%. If you borrowed an equal amount to your capital at 4% and invested it in additional loans at 7%, you would net 3% on that second batch of loans. So your total earnings on your capital would then be 7% plus 3%, or 10%. If you leveraged your capital a second time and used the money you borrowed to buy more loans, you'd make another 3%, for a total return on your capital of 7% + 3% + 3% = 13%. With every turn of leverage you'd earn another 3% of spread income.

That's how the math works, whether it is a brick-and-mortar commercial bank or a CLO, which is essentially a virtual bank, without the retail branches, loan officers, or tellers. In reality, banks and CLOs typically leverage their capital by about 9 times. Using our simple example, that would mean the equity owners' total return would be 7% on their original capital, plus 3% another nine times, or a total of 7% + 27% = 34%. Of course, if that's all there was to it, we'd all invest all our money in banks and CLOs.

What we neglected to add is that this is gross income on the portfolio, since we haven't deducted expenses, of which the most important is credit loss. If credit losses across your portfolio exceeded 3% in any one year, then that would totally wipe out the spread between your loan revenue (7%) and your cost of funds (4%), as well as the first 3% of return on your equity capital. Any extra credit loss above 3% would come directly out of the remaining income on your equity capital. And if it exceeded your current year's income on the capital, then it would come out of the equity capital itself.

That, in a nutshell, is the broad economic framework and business model of both a bank and a CLO. Table 13.1 provides a model of a typical CLO structure, in which we assume the organizers raise $50 million of equity and then leverage it nine times by borrowing an additional $450 million of debt. So there is a total of $500 million that is used to acquire senior corporate loans estimated to earn an average coupon of 7%, for total gross annual income of 7% times $500 million, or $35 million. We should caution readers that this is just a model, intended to demonstrate the structure and dynamics of a CLO, especially how its earnings and cash flow are so dependent on critical variables like (1) the coupon rates on the loans it holds, (2) the cost of the various debt tranches that make up its liabilities, and (3) the default and loss rates on its loan portfolio. We have attempted to use realistic assumptions about the yields on its loans and costs of its various liability tranches, but actual CLOs vary considerably from one another and from this model.

TABLE 13.1 Typical CLO Structure

ASSETS (US Dollars)	
Senior Secured Loans	500,000,000
Average Coupon	7.0%
Gross Annual Interest Income	35,000,000

LIABILITIES						
	% of Total	Capital Structure	Spread over LIBOR	LIBOR Base	Total Coupon	Interest Payment
AAA-Rated Tranche	64%	320,000,000	1.50%	2.5%	4.00%	12,800,000
AA-Rated Tranche	10%	50,000,000	1.90%	2.5%	4.40%	2,200,000
A-Rated Tranche	6%	30,000,000	2.50%	2.5%	5.00%	1,500,000
BBB-Rated Tranche	6%	30,000,000	3.70%	2.5%	6.20%	1,860,000
BB-Rated Tranche	4%	20,000,000	7.00%	2.5%	9.50%	1,900,000
Equity	10%	50,000,000				
Total	100%	500,000,000	Weighted Average Cost		4.50%	20,260,000

Gross Interest Rate Spread Between Loan Income and Cost of Leverage: 2.50%
Excess Interest Income After Cost of Leverage: 14,740,000
Excess Income as % of Equity Investment: 29.5%

Where CLOs get complicated is on the liability side. Just as a bank or bank holding company has a lot of different types of liabilities (checking and savings accounts, certificates of deposit, subordinated debt, preferred stock, bonds and notes issued at the holding company level, etc.), so does a CLO. Banks and CLOs maximize their profits by having as many cheap liabilities as possible. The lower your overall cost of funds, the greater the spread between what you earn on your loan portfolio and what you pay to fund it. In place of low-interest or no-interest checking and savings accounts, a CLO issues as much as it can of low-risk, highly rated, low-cost debt. The reason it is low-risk, highly rated, and low-cost is because investors who buy it are relying on a cushion of other debt (higher risk and higher cost debt) below it in the capital structure, along with the equity, to absorb any credit losses (or other losses for that matter, although credit is the primary risk).

Note in Table 13.1, the top line of the liabilities shows $320 million of AAA-rated notes. That represents 64% of the total assets of the CLO and it means the CLO could write off 36% of the value of its loans before there would be insufficient assets left to repay these notes. To put that into perspective, the typical annual loss on loan portfolios of this type is only about 1%. That's because the average default rate is 4% (even less according to some researchers) and with collateral security providing 75% recoveries (i.e., 25% losses on defaulted loans), the overall portfolio loss is 25% of 4%, or 1%.

So the AAA-rated top tranche of notes in a CLO is protected against loan losses totaling about 36 times the one-year average. Even in the great recession and market crash of 2008, the default rate barely reached 11%, which translated into a loss rate of about 2.75% after recoveries were added back in. So the AAA-rated notes are protected against losses of about 13 times the worst one-year experience we have ever seen. Being so well protected, it is no surprise they are priced more cheaply than any of the debt beneath them. As we go down through the liability side of the CLO, each tranche of debt is subordinated to the one(s) above it. That means it has a smaller cushion beneath it and has to pay a higher coupon rate. The AA-rated notes, for example, account for 10% of the value of the assets. When you add their 10% to the AAA-rated notes' 64%, it means the cushion beneath them has shrunk to 26% (i.e., 64% + 10% = 74%, and 100% − 74% leaves a cushion of 26%). That is still a huge margin and explains why these notes are also highly rated and only pay a slightly higher interest rate than the AAA notes.

As we travel down through the CLO's debt structure, we see the credit ratings drop as the amount of cushion beneath each debt tranche available to absorb losses becomes thinner. Hence the BB-rated note-holders, with nothing but the 10% equity margin between them and any loan losses, are paid a hefty 9.5% interest rate to cover the additional risk. In the corporate bond world, a rate of 9% is very high for a BB-rated credit. In fact, all the rates paid on CLO debt, from the AAA down to the BB, tend to be higher than rates paid on similarly rated corporate bond issues. This reflects the fact that many typical mainstream institutional investment managements and oversight committees still regard CLOs as somewhat exotic or "nonstandard" compared to the more traditional asset classes like ordinary stocks and bonds they are accustomed to. However, historical default rate statistics have shown CLO debt at all rating levels has had lower rates of default than similarly rated corporate bonds, so institutional investors savvy enough to have gotten up the learning curve on the asset class are earning a premium return for having done so.

This tells us that the BB-rated junior-most tranche of CLO debt is probably not all that risky compared to typical BB-rated (i.e., junk) bonds. That's because the 10% equity tranche below it is pretty protective and, absent a catastrophic turn of events in the credit markets, is unlikely to suffer losses so serious as to imperil the tranche above it.

Of course, that is good news for us Income Factory investors, because it is the equity tranche in these CLOs that we are interested in as candidates for our portfolios. Two closed-end funds that I have held in my own Income Factory for several years with good results are Oxford Lane Capital (OXLC) and Eagle Point Credit (ECC), both of which invest in the equity of CLOs. In fact, they were the first two closed-end funds to introduce CLO equity investing to the retail investment market, it previously having been limited to the institutional investing realm. Two newer funds have since joined the CLO fund community: OFS Credit Company (OCCI) and XAI Octagon Floating Rate and Alternative Income Term Trust (XFLT). All four are worth considering, although OXLC and ECC have longer track records and a history of higher distributions. That may change as the two newer funds build their asset bases and hopefully their distributions.

CLOs—Credit Losses and Equity Returns

In Table 13.2 we look at the effect of credit losses on a CLO's earnings. The goal of a CLO manager is to keep as much of the gross income from its loan portfolio as possible, after paying off the noteholders, and be able to pass it down to the CLO's equity owners. That means keeping loan losses to a minimum, through good due diligence up front (i.e., buying the right loans) and careful monitoring and management of the portfolio throughout the life of the CLO.

We saw in Table 13.1 that our model CLO had $14,740,000 of gross earnings, after paying off its noteholders but prior to deducting loan losses or other expenses, to distribute down to its equity. Absent any losses or other expenses, that would be a gross return to equity of over 29%. In Table 13.2 we show the impact of average credit losses on that return. The high-yield loan market has averaged about 4% defaults for many years. Since the loans are secured with collateral, the average recovery on a defaulted loan has been 75%, resulting in an average loss of 25%. If 4% of our portfolio defaults, and we average losses of 25% on each defaulted loan, the resulting portfolio-wide loss is 25% times 4%, or 1%.

TABLE 13.2 Average Credit Loss Scenario

Projected Default Rate	4%
Projected Recovery Rate on Defaulted Loans	75%
Projected Loss Rate on Defaulted Loans	25%
Projected Portfolio Loss Rate	1%
Projected Portfolio Credit Loss	5,000,000
Net Income After Credit Losses	9,740,000
Net Income as % of Equity Investment	19.5%

Deducting 1% for loan losses from the portfolio-wide spread on our loans has the effect of decreasing the earnings that would otherwise accrue to the equity owners by 1% times $500 million, which is $5,000,000. That reduces the earnings to $9,740,000, which is a return of 19.5%, down from a gross return of 29.5%. That is what we would expect, since a 1% credit cost multiplied by 10 (i.e., the equity plus nine turns of leverage) results in a total charge of 10% to the equity, since the equity has to absorb all the credit losses across the entire portfolio. For equity investors, the knowledge that a typical CLO could absorb average credit default levels of 4% and still have 19.5% to pay other expenses and our equity distributions is good news.

TABLE 13.3 Pessimistic Credit Loss Scenario

Projected Default Rate	8%
Projected Recovery Rate	75%
Projected Loss Rate on Defaulted Loans	25%
Projected Portfolio Loss Rate	2%
Projected Portfolio Credit Loss	10,000,000
Net Income After Credit Losses	4,740,000
Net Income as % of Equity Investment	9.5%

   In Table 13.3 we kick it up a notch and assume a default rate that is double the average, or 8%. This results in a portfolio-wide credit loss of 2%, which with the impact of 9 times leverage on top of the equity means the equity holders have to absorb a 10 times 2%, or 20%, hit to their earnings margin. This drops the return on equity to 9.5%. It shows the resilience of both senior secured loans as an asset class and of the CLO structure that the equity could absorb a 2% portfolio-wide credit loss hit (twice the historical average) that translates into a 20% equity hit and still provide a return in the 9% range, before other expenses. (At least, with these assumptions. As mentioned, every CLO is different and markets change, as do all of the assumptions we have built into our model.)

   In Table 13.4 we stress our model CLO even further and assume a draconian default rate of 12%, which is worse than the level reached in the great recession of 2008. Even at that elevated default rate, while our CLO model would have to forego its annual distribution to equity investors, it would still remain financially solvent and be able to return to its more normal level of distributions in future years.

TABLE 13.4 Draconian Credit Loss Scenario

Projected Default Rate	12%
Projected Recovery Rate	75%
Projected Loss Rate on Defaulted Loans	25%
Projected Portfolio Loss Rate	3.00%
Projected Portfolio Credit Loss	15,000,000
Net Income After Credit Losses	−260,000
Net Income as % of Equity Investment	−0.5%

That is essentially what happened in the past. CLOs, as an asset class, managed to survive the financial crash in good shape, with investors who sat tight and held their positions achieving very attractive returns even despite some temporary drops in cash flow. Offsetting the cash-flow drops was the opportunity to reinvest incoming cash at bargain prices, since many of the 90% or more of healthy, performing loans were being priced in the market at about 60 cents on the dollar. This allowed CLOs and other loan investors to put new money (mostly principal repayments) to work at bargain prices and yields, boosting overall returns.

It is this durability and performance "under fire" that has made CLOs an attractive investment vehicle to so many institutional investors over many years and more recently to some of us retail investors. But they are not for the faint-hearted and involve a fair amount of work to stay on top of all the detail and complexity. In return for that the closed-end funds that own them pay us distributions in the midteens, which helps spice up the overall yield on our Income Factories.

CLOs—Cash Flows and Distributions

The "waterfall" of cash flows in a CLO, as displayed in Table 13.5, is pretty simple and straightforward. There is all this cash—interest payments and principal repayments—that flows in from the CLO's borrowers, the companies whose loans it holds in its portfolio. The incoming cash is used first to repay the most senior creditors of the CLO, the AAA-rated noteholders. After they are paid, then the remaining cash is distributed to the other noteholders in turn again by seniority, until we get to the end of the line where the owners of the CLO, the equity holders, receive whatever is left.

TABLE 13.5 CLO Cash-Flow "Waterfall"

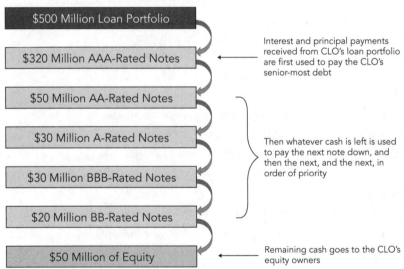

When we consider the waterfall chart, it actually describes pretty closely what happens in a real bank in terms of the various claims against the cash that is collected from the bank's loan portfolio. On the asset side of the bank, the revenues come in from the loans and other assets the bank owns, just as a CLO collects revenue from its loan portfolio. Bank liabilities typically are tiered as well with checking, savings, and other deposits first in line for payment and various types of long-term debt (especially if it is at the holding company level), convertible securities, and preferred stock further down the list of bank liabilities. Then at the very end of the line comes the equity.

Banks, just like CLOs, have to pay their liabilities (deposit accounts and other debt) regardless of whether their own borrowers pay them back or not. Just because a borrower defaults doesn't give the bank the right to take it out of my checking account. Those losses all come out of the equity. If losses are so great they eat up all of the equity, then it works its way up through the preferred stock and subordinated debt, only in rare cases reaching the deposits and senior liabilities. Long before that, the federal or state banking authorities would usually step in and arrange a merger or some other sort of controlled liquidation.

A CLO works much the same way, and while there is no depositor safety net or equivalent to protect investors, the record of CLOs in avoiding defaults over several decades is very strong. But essentially, the overall economics of a CLO—who takes the risks and what factors influence the returns they receive—are very similar to that of a bank, once you cut through the securitization jargon with its references to tranches and waterfalls. That's why I think it is easier to understand a CLO if you think of it as a virtual bank, although I have seldom seen it described that way elsewhere.

In reality, it would be rare for a CLO to experience loan losses so great that they would wipe out the CLO's equity capital. In fact, 50% of all CLOs over the past two decades have generated returns in excess of 15% for their equity investors, and only 4% of them have failed to generate at least a positive return. There are no guarantees the future will be like the past, so the way we protect ourselves going forward, whether investing in real banks or in CLOs, is through diversification. As retail investors, our main means of investing in CLOs is through funds, where the funds themselves are well diversified and own the equity of dozens of CLOs. In our draconian example earlier, we stressed our model by assuming credit defaults at the highest level experienced over the past four decades, and while it wiped out the current income of the equity tranche, the equity capital itself was untouched and would have been pumping out cash again the following year.

CLOs: Safe but Complicated

While it may be safe (remember *safe* is a relative term for an asset that yields in the midteens), CLO equity can be complicated, especially identifying and labeling the cash flow received from it. Is it income? Is it return of capital (ROC)? Is it "good" ROC or "bad" ROC? What is the real return on my CLO equity, and how long can I expect to keep earning it?

Most investors, including myself, will never be experts on all these complicated topics, but we can at least be aware of the issues and be prepared to ask the right questions about the funds we are considering in the CLO space. And the number one topic that requires analysis and explanation is cash flow. As we have seen, generating cash flow is the essential purpose of a CLO. The whole idea in structuring a CLO is to acquire a portfolio of loans and maximize the cash flows it produces, while financing that portfolio as economically as possible through an optimal blend of a whole lot of low-risk, low-priced liabilities and a smaller portion of higher-risk, more-expensive liabilities. The goal is to maximize the spread or margin between the incoming and outgoing fund flows, since that margin—after deducting credit losses and administrative expenses—is what flows down to the equity investors.

The challenge is categorizing the cash that flows down to the equity, so we are not overstating or understating the amount of it that represents profit as opposed to merely a return of our principal. Credit losses are the biggest single factor that can disrupt the cash flow to equity. As noted previously, a 1% write-off across the entire portfolio represents a 10% hit to equity on a portfolio whose assets, through leverage, are 10 times the amount of the equity. A 2% portfolio-wide write-off becomes a 20% hit to equity, and so on.

Identifying credit losses and properly accounting for them is tricky. If you are overly conservative and overaccrue for losses, you understate your net earnings to your equity owners. But if you underaccrue for losses, you mislead your equity owners into thinking they are making more money than they really are, and they are disappointed later on when they find out there are losses buried in the portfolio that were never recognized and accrued.

The tax laws don't make this any easier, because they require closed-end funds to pay out virtually all of their income to their shareholders on a regular basis. They also only allow tax deductions for loan losses when the loans are finally written off and the loss recognized, not for a loan loss accrual a year or so earlier that anticipates a loss that will not occur until sometime in the future. Since lightning can strike anytime over the 8- to 10-year life of a typical CLO, it is prudent credit management and also good GAAP accounting for a fund owning CLOs to accrue for credit losses over time, thus accumulating a reserve that it can tap to absorb losses when they occur, rather than waiting for defaults and losses to just occur randomly and play havoc with the fund's reported earnings.

A fund owning CLO equity that does that and accrues for credit losses every year will probably have some years where there are no losses, especially early in the life of the CLOs it holds, when the loans are newer and whatever problems that eventually cause the borrower to default have not arisen yet. That means the cash flow the fund receives from the CLO those years will be greater than its reported GAAP profit, which will have been reduced by the accrual of the non-cash charge for credit losses, effectively building up a reserve for future years as described earlier.

Instead of effectively building up a reserve for future losses, a fund may decide (or be required by tax regulations) to distribute more than its GAAP earnings to shareholders, hoping the credit loss estimates it used in developing its GAAP earnings model were overly pessimistic and that loss rates would remain lower. In that case the fund risks having an insufficient reserve if future losses appear after all, forcing it to either (1) lower its distribution or (2) invade the fund's net asset value to maintain the distribution at its previous level.

Some funds compromise and pay the higher dividend in the early years, but break it into two pieces, labeling the more sustainable portion of it as the "regular dividend" and then paying a "special dividend" on top of it, thus creating less of an expectation that the total will be continued indefinitely. This option is frequently used when what the fund regards as temporary or one-time cash flows push its taxable income to a point where the minimum required payout (generally 90% for closed-end funds) is greater than what the fund regards as its sustainable distribution level. A special or one-time distribution allows the fund to meet its tax requirements while also signaling to its shareholders not to expect such a generous payout every year, thus avoiding disappointment and the market price drops that might accompany it. It is not a perfect solution, in that the fund may still be using "windfall" cash flow that it will end up wishing it still had later on when or if credit losses finally arise. But at least it allows itself to limit such a windfall cash-flow expenditure to a single year, rather than create a precedent for doing it every year.

Confused Yet? Well, There's More

When a closed-end fund pays out more than its normal investment income (i.e., its GAAP accounting income) as part of its distribution to shareholders, the excess portion of the distribution is called a return of capital (ROC). An ROC like that previously described, where you are depleting a reserve you may need later to take credit losses, can come back to bite you later and is sometimes referred to as a "destructive" ROC. What makes investing in closed-end funds interesting and— at times—challenging, is that there are many other types of ROC that are not destructive, and it is often difficult to discern between the destructive and constructive categories. This is particularly true of closed-end funds that buy CLO equity.

As we noted earlier, funds that buy CLO equity are frequently going to receive back more cash flow than they can prudently count as income under normal GAAP accounting standards. At the same time they are encouraged and/or required by tax laws to distribute most of that gross cash flow to shareholders. That sets up sort of a bias toward including a certain amount of ROC that may be of the potentially destructive variety in a fund's distributions almost as a matter of course. This could lead to a constant, steady erosion of the fund's net asset value over the course of its life, if credit losses within the CLO fail to fully match up with and get provided for on the books of the fund.

Fund managers, knowing this, have ways to offset this erosion of their funds' net asset value (NAV) and *build par* over the course of time. Many of these tactics for building par generate capital gains or write-ups in the value of their portfolios and are therefore reported as ROC when distributed to shareholders. This constructive ROC can offset destructive ROC, so as a shareholder when you see that one of your funds is reporting a certain percentage of its distribution as ROC, you don't always know whether it is constructive or destructive.

Some ways that fund managers and/or the CLO managers can build par and offset the negative effects of destructive ROC include:

- Buying their equity at a discount to begin with. Many times CLO originators, in constructing the CLO and realizing that CLO equity is a highly illiquid and complex investment, discount the equity portion to induce original investors to buy it. That means the investor (i.e., like our closed-end fund) goes into the deal with a built-in capital gain, available to partially offset future erosion of capital.
- Astute trading in and out of their funds' loan portfolios. Loans that may be perfectly healthy in terms of meeting their interest and principal payments can still move up and down in the loan market, so CLO managers try to be vigilant in looking for opportunities to upgrade their portfolios, improve their margins, and take capital gains, which go into the constructive ROC category.
- "Resetting" the terms of the CLO, which pushes out its maturity and allows the fund manager additional years to reinvest principal payments received on maturing loans, rather than having to wind down the CLO according to its original terms. Every additional year a manager can maintain a CLO at its full initial size without starting the wind-down process means additional full-margin earnings for equity owners.

- Similarly, fund managers can renegotiate the terms of their liabilities (even without extending the life of the CLO) if market conditions shift in the borrowers' favor (lower spreads for AAA debt, etc.). This can cut both ways, of course, if the CLO's own borrowers decide to prepay their loans to get cheaper funding elsewhere.

- While it may seem counterintuitive, periods of loan market turbulence can be particularly good times for CLOs to build par. That's because the cash flows continue even though market prices, for the loans themselves and for the CLO equity, may be dropping. That allows CLO managers to put repayments or any other new money to work at bargain prices, boosting future spreads and income.

It may be obvious to readers at this point that the return investors receive from investing in CLOs (whether large institutional investors who buy equity directly in individual CLOs, or retail investors like us who buy CLO equity via funds) is a moving target and that the distributions we receive are made up partly of yield and partly of return of capital. And we won't necessarily know how much is which until sometime later.

Besides everything we have already discussed, there is one more big reason for this lack of certainty. It relates to the internal dynamics of a CLO's unique structure. Recall how a CLO's liability structure is carefully balanced between a lot of cheap highly rated debt and a smaller buffer of expensive lower-rated debt, designed to provide an optimal overall cost of funds significantly lower than the average interest rate on the loans on the asset side of the CLO's balance sheet. This spread between the CLO's cost of funds and what it collects from its loan portfolio is the lifeblood of the entire CLO.

Once a CLO reaches its amortization stage, where the manager no longer has the option of reinvesting principal received from the CLO's loan portfolio, then the principal has to be used to pay off the CLO's own debt. Of course the AAA-rated debt gets paid off first, then the AA debt, then the BBBs, and so on. With every dollar of cheap AAA debt that is repaid, the average cost of funds increases and the CLO's profit margin shrinks. As the AAA, AA, and other debt gets paid off, eventually the only debt left would be debt that costs as much or more than some of the loans on the asset side. At that point the CLO would become a losing proposition. A smart CLO manager wants to avoid this, either by "resetting" the CLO so that the wind-down date is pushed out into the future and they can keep on reinvesting the principal repayments in new loans, or by accelerating the wind-down and selling off all the loans and repaying all the debts at once or within a very narrow time period.

Whether a CLO is reset or not, at some point it will be time to wind it down and that will usually involve putting the entire portfolio of loans, many of them seasoned, older loans with perhaps just a few years left to run, up for sale. By then the portfolio may be a mixed bag, with most loans performing as expected, some performing so well their credit ratings have been upgraded, and others identified as potential problems. And some of the portfolio will be gone, in the sense that it consisted of loans that made earlier prepayments that were used to pay distributions. In other words, it is capital that has already been returned to shareholders, albeit as part of a distribution.

The upshot of this is that the fund may take a capital loss, of some amount, when many of their CLO positions are liquidated. Whether the various opportunistic actions the fund managers take to build par offset the erosion that can occur over time as CLOs are liquidated at a capital loss and/or capital leaks out as part of the distribution stream is a big question for any of these funds.

Knowing What to Watch For

The purpose of this has not been to make readers experts in CLO accounting, but rather to provide an idea of what issues to watch for and focus on if you decide to spice up your Income Factory with CLO funds, which I and many other Income Factory adherents have chosen to do. It mostly involves closely examining these funds' reports and presentations to try to get as clear a picture as possible of the sustain-ability of their distributions and the cash flows underlying them. Even if we are not accountants or professional analysts, we can:

- Read reports and listen to presentations carefully to deter-mine how much of any fund's distribution is comprised of "real earnings" for the period, which many investors would probably consider net investment income (i.e., interest and other pay-ments received that do *not* include principal repayments) and realized capital gains. The more of the distribution that is cov-ered by discernible earnings, the less we have to worry about our distributions representing a partial erosion of our own invested capital.
- If the distribution does contain some ROC, then we should look for information about what the ROC component consists of, and if we don't see it, ask the question at the fund's quarterly earnings presentation.
- We should also monitor closely the fund's price versus its dis-tribution yield. Nothing tells us more about whether the ROC portion of a fund's distribution is constructive or destructive than the fund's longer-term stock price trend. If the fund can pay out a distribution of, say, 14% and its stock price retains its value over time, then we would conclude that whatever ROC the distribution contains, it is most likely constructive, since it doesn't seem to be eroding the market's estimate of the fund's underlying value.
- On the other hand, if the price seems to be steadily giving up 1% or 2% of its market value, year after year, then we would likely conclude that its capital value (its net asset value, or NAV) is eroding at that rate because of destructive ROC. That doesn't necessarily mean it is a bad investment, since a distribution of 14% of which 11% or 12% was its true yield and the rest was capital erosion might still be a very attractive asset in one's Income Factory. The key is to understand what is going on and be aware of it.

- Besides monitoring the sources of our funds' distributions over the long term, we should also focus on the funds' shorter-term capacity to continue meeting its current distribution, regardless of its sources. Funds often signal to investors what their intentions are in this regard, either explicitly by declaring several months of distributions in advance or by stating clearly that their cash flow is sufficient to meet the current level of distributions plus other fund expenses. As an investor, it is comforting to get this sort of reassurance, especially if the fund also addresses its longer-term plans for funding the distribution in a manner that does not erode its permanent capital. And if it does not address it, we should raise the question with fund management.

Final Thoughts on CLOs

Institutional investors have invested in CLOs for decades, with excellent results, even through the great recession of 2008. Unfortunately, many retail investors confuse the name, mistaking CLOs for the CDOs (collateralized debt obligations) that held subprime mortgage loans, so-called liar's loans from people with either no or phony credit histories, and other marginal security (including pieces of previous CDOs that had failed to sell the first time around) and which helped precipitate the crash.

So it has been an uphill battle for the industry to market itself to the retail public. Making it harder has been all the complexity we have already described, plus the somewhat artificial requirement that funds that hold CLO equity have to calculate (estimate) a net asset value periodically for an asset class that has no transparent market with easily discernible prices. For most of its 30-year history, CLOs were bought and held by institutional investors who could buy them, hold them in portfolio and calculate a specific return for each CLO based on its cash flows, without having to worry about marking them to market. Closed-end funds and other funds that own CLOs do not have that luxury.

All of this presents an opportunity for retail investors to collect a premium return if they are willing to learn about CLOs and to live with the lack of certainty and transparency that they present, which normal stocks, bonds, and mutual funds do not. So far, it has been worth it, with many investors, like myself, having been able to pocket and reinvest the entire distribution with only negligible capital erosion. Will that continue in the future? I don't know but will be watching the funds closely and asking management the sort of questions outlined here.

From Benjamin Graham to the Income Factory

The Income Factory was initially regarded as a heretical upstart in the world of investment theories and philosophies. But as more investors come to understand it better, I believe many will conclude that it is a logical extension of the fundamental investment tradition extending back to Benjamin Graham and the original proponents of value-driven investing.

If we follow the development of that tradition, we see the inexorable march toward achieving equity returns in the cheapest, simplest, and most predictable manner. Investors came to realize that no matter how much original fundamental research they did on public companies, it was virtually impossible to gain insight or understanding that was not already "baked into" the market price of the companies' stock. The road led eventually to equity indexing, which makes total sense but does not eliminate the need for strong wills and steel nerves during market downturns.

The Income Factory goes a step further in recognizing (1) that the ability to produce income is what ultimately determines the economic value of one's investment portfolio and (2) achieving market price growth is not a necessary part of that process.

Removing the market price growth requirement opens up the option of achieving an "equity return" without actually holding equities, while also eliminating much of the angst and drama that accompanies many investors' endless concern with market price movements.

* * *

The Income Factory philosophy initially may seem to be outside the traditional investing mainstream. On closer examination, I think many investors will see that it draws on many of the mainstream's core valuation principles and will be attracted to a thoughtful, alternative approach aimed at achieving the same long-term results with less volatility.

Most serious retail investors, who have grown up on the fundamental investing philosophy of Graham and Dodd, Warren Buffett, and John Bogle, know—intellectually—that a long-term, buy-and-hold equity strategy (whether indexed or otherwise) is best. But they find—emotionally—that the volatile short-term ups and downs are more than they can handle. Their left brain may say, "Wait, let's ride it out," while their right brain says, "Let's get out of here!" Many of these investors welcome a steadier, more predictable approach based on income growth rather than market price growth.

Beyond the well-informed investor who is familiar with the traditional investing "canon" is a massive retail audience that the investment radio networks and other popular media cultivate, of investors scared to death of equities, especially after the 2008 crash. This is the group most likely to fall for all the pitches for annuities and other products that offer "guaranteed returns" of 5% or 6% or so. The Income Factory approach offers these investors the option of creating their own annuity-like income stream that can add another 1%, 2%, or more to their returns (while saving a lot of fees) that will ultimately double or triple their income stream (or more, compared to an annuity or equivalent) over a lifetime of investing.

The canon of mainstream investment books begins with Benjamin Graham and David Dodd's *Security Analysis* (1934). This created the analytical framework we still use to value stocks and to identify those that Graham's "Mr. Market" (an allegory he created) misprices too cheaply and therefore represent "value" to potential investors. Graham's later writings took the framework and made it a bit more accessible for the nonacademic reader. Prior to Graham and Dodd's work, investing—for the average investor, professional, or amateur—was more of a gambling exercise, with no broad underlying theory of value to explain or justify market prices. This made the ultimate crash, when it came in 1929 and thereafter, even harsher than it would have been otherwise.

At about the same time, John Burr Williams published his lesser-known but profoundly important book *The Theory of Investment Value* (1938), which introduced the idea of a security's value being the sum of its discounted future cash flows. These ideas, Graham and Dodd's and Williams's together, underpin many of the mainstream investment strategies developed over the next half century. The Income Factory focuses on high-income securities, both stocks and credit instruments. But it draws heavily on Williams's basic theme, especially the idea that "cash flows are cash flows," whatever their source, for purposes of calculating an investment's present value, and distributions and dividends therefore count just as much in the value equation as anticipated future growth.

Several decades later, Princeton professor Burton Malkiel published his classic *A Random Walk Down Wall Street* (1973), which downplays the value of "fundamental" analysis of the Graham and Dodd variety. Malkiel proposes instead an "efficient-market hypothesis" that claims the additional insight gained by a value analysis is already known to the market and incorporated into the price of the security.

By now most thoughtful investment experts realize it is hardly an "either-or" choice between the two camps. Many commentators, including index fund pioneer John Bogle, who founded Vanguard Investments and started the first publicly available index fund, have been inclined to blend both investment philosophies, accepting the basic idea that "fundamentals" do indeed determine stock values, while acknowledging that the market "bakes" new data into stock prices faster than most investors can analyze it and act upon it.

Of course, the goal of indexing or "random walk" investing is to match the long-term equity return at the lowest possible cost. Most of the cost we hear about from proponents of indexing has to do with trading costs and other fees associated with actively managing one's portfolio, but the far bigger cost that afflicts so many equity investors—whether indexers or more active ones—is the cost associated with losing one's nerve and exiting the market during down periods. Being on the sidelines when the growth train starts up again and pulls out of the station costs investors many times as much as the savings they get from holding low-cost index funds.

This is not an argument against index funds, which make total sense for long-term investors capable of buying their index funds and then holding on through thick and thin for many years to reap the benefits. The problem isn't with the funds, but rather with investors who don't stick with the program. Famed money manager Charles Ellis made this point in his classic book *Winning the Loser's Game* in which he compares investing to amateur tennis, where more points are lost by making bad shots than are won by making winners. The "bad shots" most amateur (and some professional) money managers make are their attempts to either beat or time the market, rather than accept an average equity return achieved as economically as possible through indexing.

Several messages come through clearly, from Graham and Dodd, Williams, Malkiel, Bogle, Ellis, and others. One is that the fundamentals are important and do indeed drive stock prices. Another is the markets have now become such an efficient, zero-sum game that fundamental data is absorbed by the market and incorporated into stock prices before individual investors can act upon it. Therefore, it is not worth an investor's while to try to beat the market, and achieving the long-run average return at the least cost—indexing—is the best strategy. If anyone has any doubts about whether following such a strategy is worth it, they should read Jeremy Siegel's book *Stocks for the*

Long Run. Siegel's book makes the case for essentially following the advice of the other authors cited, demonstrating the wealth-building power of equities for the past 200 years.

The Income Factory takes this theme to the next step and provides a practical alternative. It recognizes that many investors do not have the personal confidence, willpower, and nerves of steel required to steadfastly hold a stock portfolio, indexed or otherwise, through all sorts of market conditions over many decades. Those that do have the requisite willpower and other qualities have many options: indexing, dividend growth investing, or more actively managed portfolios, mutual funds, and other vehicles.

The Income Factory is for those who prefer not to put themselves to the test of having to watch their portfolios plunge during market reversals without the offsetting comfort of having a river of cash to reinvest at bargain prices and sky-high yields. Why buy stocks at all, they ask, if buying stocks is a zero-sum game where the best you can do is match the average result of the entire market, and there is an easier alternative? The Income Factory gives them a choice to achieve that equity return in less-volatile asset classes, minus the angst and drama.

APPENDIX

Financial Innovation

A Case Study

If there are some overarching themes of this book, they might include (1) the role of credit and fixed income as important but often underrated building blocks in an equity-return strategy, and (2) the importance of being open-minded to new approaches to old challenges, regardless of how radical they may first appear.

To provide a bit of additional "color" for readers interested in some of the inner workings of credit investing and analysis, and to show how random and idiosyncratic the whole process of financial innovation can be, we are republishing here an article that originally appeared on the Seeking Alpha site in 2015, on the peculiar circumstances that resulted in the introduction of credit ratings to the corporate loan industry.

* * *

Today it is hard to imagine a robust syndicated loan market without widespread distribution of major loans to an extensive investor base of banks, endowments, pensions, mutual funds, hedge funds, and, especially, securitized vehicles like collateralized loan obligations (CLOs).

It is equally difficult to imagine a healthy loan market without a system for rating loans and classifying them in terms of their default and recovery expectations, with links to the historical data that underpin those ratings and maps to the capital and reserve requirements of the banks and their regulators.

So it may seem like the "dark ages" of credit and lending to think back almost 30 years and reflect on a loan market without credit ratings, where the link between pricing and risk was tenuous. Many old-time "commercial" bankers (like the author) recall when banks used to hold their loans to maturity on their own books, and how credit analysis focused on a simple "yes/no" decision. Should we make the loan? Did the deal meet the bank's credit standards? There was little "portfolio management" in the decision. And pricing, especially, was an afterthought. Credit was all: is this deal a good one or a bad one?

In joining Standard & Poor's in 1992, I certainly had no notion of being a missionary to bring ratings to the commercial banking heathen. In fact, at that time the market that was considered ripe for picking by the rating agencies was the private placement market (corporate bonds and notes privately placed with insurance companies). The insurance regulator, the National Association of Insurance Commissioners, had just adopted a new credit scale that featured a huge reserve "cliff" between investment grade (BBB– and above) and non-investment grade (BB+ and below) borrowers, thus providing a potential inroad for ratings to help define which deals made the cut and which didn't.

Loans at a Private Placement Conference

So it was that in pursuit of the goal of penetrating that market I found myself in 1993 at an institutional private placement conference in New York. Loans had not yet generated enough interest among nonbank investors to support entire conferences devoted to them. But awareness had grown to the point where panel discussions on loans had begun to appear on the agenda of private placement conferences, usually sandwiched into the last half of the second day, where they competed for the audience's attention with the hotel bar and the early train home to Greenwich. As a result, there was not much of an audience left to witness the incident I will now relate, which figured so mightily in the development of loan ratings.

This particular panel on loans featured James B. (Jimmy) Lee, Jr. At the time Lee was running Chemical Bank's powerhouse syndicated lending group, from which he went on to head the bank's investment banking group, and ultimately to become vice-chairman of JP Morgan Chase. Known and admired throughout the financial world, Lee was a legend in the syndicated loan industry. While the rest of the panel's membership and presentation was pretty forgettable, Lee's answer to one of the questions from the audience was memorable, and catalytic in its impact on me, on S&P, and on the loan rating business. Asked by an audience member, "How do you price your loans?" Jimmy didn't hesitate a nanosecond before answering, "We price 'em all the same—400 basis points over LIBOR." The audience chuckled and that was it, on to the next question.

But Lee's comment, partly in jest, but with a big grain of truth in it, gnawed at me for days afterward. I knew syndicated corporate loans were essentially a non-investment grade market that included double-B, single-B, and even triple-C borrowers. At S&P we knew from decades of default statistics that single-B companies defaulted two to three times as often as double-B firms, and that default rates really jumped in triple-C territory. I also knew that in the bond and private placement worlds, the pricing "cliffs" between triple-B, double-B, single-B, and triple-C were huge. So if Jimmy Lee's remark were even remotely true, then corporate treasurers and institutional investors were continually leaving money on the table or getting a windfall from one deal to another, depending on where each issuer fell on the credit spectrum.

Now you would think, armed with authoritative, actionable market intelligence like this, straight from the horse's mouth, that we at S&P would have jumped all over it. Unfortunately, S&P didn't have a rating that would work too well in evaluating secured loans to non-investment grade borrowers. Our traditional business had been rating corporate bonds, which were unsecured and issued mostly by investment grade companies. The whole analytical focus was on the risk of default. In other words, what was the likelihood of the issuer failing to pay interest or principal on time? Period. Since the chance of that occurring with investment grade issuers was minimal, there was almost never any collateral security to evaluate or much reason to analyze what would happen in a "post-default" environment. (The advent of high-yield bonds changed that, but only a little. They were unsecured or even subordinated, so when defaults came, as they often did, there was little to recover.)

"No Rating" Is Better Than a Bad Rating

As long as a rating only addressed default risk, a rating on a bank loan was no help at all. It only emphasized the negative (that high-yield companies were prone to default); not the positive (that when they did default, secured lenders got most of their money back). But commercial bankers have always known how to make a risky credit "bankable" by tying the borrower up with protective covenants and collateral security. Although it represented a major change from past practice, S&P's criteria and methodology gurus eventually agreed with us that a "dual risk" approach—default risk *and* expected recovery—was necessary if we wanted to serve the bank loan market. It also helped that the bankers S&P went out and talked to reaffirmed to us over and over again that such a two-dimensional approach was absolutely necessary.

The rest is history. S&P introduced "recovery ratings" to complement its traditional default ratings, and other rating agencies developed their own methodologies to address the issue. Rating syndicated loans became an integral part of S&P's corporate rating business, with volume some years even exceeding traditional corporate bond ratings. Now, almost three decades later, we might well ask:

How could anyone *not* analyze the structure, security, and loss/recovery prospects of a company's various debt issues as separate elements of rating the total company? The answer may seem obvious today, but it certainly was not back then when Jimmy Lee took that question from the audience and helped spark a mini-revolution in the analysis of corporate credit.

Index

Page numbers followed by *f* and *t* refer to figures and tables, respectively.

AAA corporate bonds, 169–170, 191
AFT (Apollo Floating Rate), 120
Age, of investors, 47, 65
Aggressive investing/investors, 67–68, 113–118
Aggressive risk/reward profile—12 funds, 109–111, 110*t*
Aggressive risk/reward profile—20 funds, 112–113, 112*t*
AGIC Convertible and Income Funds, 96
AIF (Apollo Tactical Income), 95
Amortization stage, of CLOs, 202–203
Analysis:
    credit, 180–181
    fundamental, 209
    for stock market, 24
Annuities, 21, 128
Apollo Floating Rate (AFT), 120
Apollo Tactical Income (AIF), 95
Asset classes:
    diversification between and among, 90–91
    with fixed income, 155–157
    flexibility of options in, 97
    funds from, 13
    higher yields as normal in, 129–130
    for Income Factory, 89–90, 90*t*
    in investment selection, 82–86
    in model portfolios, 110

risk/reward profile of different, 157–161
selection of, for taxable accounts, 81–82
senior loans, 180–182
specialized, 72
stretching for yield in different, 128–130
structured, 72

B corporate bonds, 171–172
Balanced income/growth model portfolio, 50, 51*t*, 52
Banks:
    cash flow and distributions in, 196–197
    correspondent, 181
    credit analysis performed by, 180–181
    virtual, 187–188
Barings Corporate Investors (MCI), 95
Barings Global Short Duration (BGH), 95
BB corporate bonds, 171, 192
BBB corporate bonds, 169–171
BDCs (business development companies), 101, 130, 156
Benchmarks, 23–25
Berra, Yogi, 186
BGH (Barings Global Short Duration), 95
BGX (Blackstone/GSO Strategic Credit), 111

Black Rock Corporate High Yield
(HYT), 120
Black Rock Debt Strategies (DSU), 120
Blackstone/GSO Strategic Credit (BGX),
111
Blue chip stocks, 47
Bogle, John, 208, 209–210
Bonds:
credit rating scales for, 171–172
low yield of, 128
traditional, 166–169
(*See also* corporate bonds)
Brookfield Asset Management group, 96
Brookfield Real Assets (RA), 96
BTO (John Hancock Financial
Opportunities), 102, 123
Buffett, Warren, 208
Business development companies
(BDCs), 101, 130, 156
Business performance, 32
Buybacks, 38

Calamos Convertible & High Income
(CHY), 122
Calamos Strategic Total Return (CSQ),
96, 122
Capital gains, 104
Capital structure, 178
Cash flows, 196–197
CBRE Clarion Global Real Estate (IGR),
122
CDOs (collateralized debt obligations),
75, 130, 205
CDs, low yield of, 128
CEF Connect website, 136
CHY (Calamos Convertible & High
Income), 122
CIK (Credit Suisse Asset Management
Income), 120
CLOs (*see* Collateralized loan obligations
(CLOs))
Closed-end funds:
equity-covered call funds as, 102
as fixed income, 156
higher yield as typical in, 130
as high-yield investments, 83
liquidity risk of, 73–74

senior loans in, 186
stretching for yield with, 130–132
tax advantaged, 146–147
in taxable accounts, 82
in ultra-high-yield strategies, 134–135
Cohen & Steers Closed End Opportunity
(FOF), 96, 122
Cohen & Steers Infrastructure (UTF),
100
Cohen & Steers Limited Duration
Preferred & Income Fund (LDP),
122
Collateralized debt obligations (CDOs),
75, 130, 205
Collateralized loan obligations (CLOs),
14–15, 187–206
cash flows and distributions in,
196–197
complexity risk of, 75–76
credit loss on, 193*t*–195*t*
credit losses and equity returns on,
193–195
doing your research on, 203–205
as fixed income, 156
historical performance of, 186, 197
and income, 188–192
safety and complexity of, 198–200
structure of, 189–190, 190*t*
in ultra-high-yield strategies, 134–135
uncertainty in, 200–203
Complexity:
of assets, 135
of collateralized loan obligations,
198–200
Complexity risk, 74–76, 78
Compounding:
growth provided by, 2, 44–45
power of, 5
and Rule of 72, 35–36
in tax-advantaged vs. taxable accounts,
80–82
Convertible bond funds, 93*t*, 97
Convertible securities, 156
Corporate bond funds, 71
Corporate bonds:
and credit risk, 169–170
default rates of, 170*t*

high-yield, 166
investment grade, 166
Corporate loan funds, 71–72
Corporate stock funds, 71, 83
Correspondent banks, 181
Credit analysis, 180–181
Credit loss(es), 179
    calculations of, 182–185, 183t, 184t
    in collateralized loan obligations,
        193–195
    on collateralized loan obligations,
        193t–195t
    identifying and accounting for,
        198–199
Credit rating scales:
    for bonds, 171–172
    in collateralized loan obligations, 191
    for loans, 181–182
    as two-dimensional, 213–217
Credit risk, 76–77, 159, 161t
    and corporate bonds, 169–170
    for high-yield bonds, 172–173
    for stocks, 174
    of stocks, 161–163
    on traditional bonds, 166–169
Credit Suisse Asset Management Income
    (CIK), 120
CSQ (Calamos Strategic Total Return),
    96, 122

Debt instruments, 166, 167t
Deep moats, 100
Default:
    in collateralized loan obligations,
        193–196
    loss vs., 179–180
    rates of, for corporate bonds, 170t
    risk of, and credit rating, 178
Deferred taxes, 79
Defined benefit pensions, 20–21
Defined contribution retirement plans,
    21–22
Destructive ROC, 200–201
DFH (Dreyfus High Yield Strategies),
    120
Discount:
    buying equity at, 201

closed-end funds purchased at,
    130–131
Distributions:
    from collateralized loan obligations,
        204–205
    in collateralized loan obligations,
        196–197
    diversification to reduce risks of cuts in,
        111, 114–115
    as economic value of asset, 25
    as element of total return, 31–32
    portfolio growth through, 11
    reinvestment of, 16–17
Diversification:
    among investment managers, 72, 103
    between and in asset classes, 90–91
    to counter risk, 54
    mitigating risks with, 55, 71, 78
    in ultra-high-yield strategies, 133–134
Dividend growth:
    and price/earnings ratio, 36–37
    and stock price growth, 33–36
Dividend growth investing, 27, 29,
    33, 45
Dividend growth stock:
    for Income Factory Light, 141–142,
        142t
    in taxable accounts, 149–151
Dividends:
    atypically high, 128–129
    paid by collateralized loan obligations,
        199–200
    as portion of total returns, 23
Dodd, David, 24, 208, 209
"Do-it-yourself kit" model, 143–145,
    143t
Donald Duck comic books, 21
Dreyfus High Yield Strategies (DFH),
    120
DSU (Black Rock Debt Strategies), 120

Eagle Point Credit (ECC), 134–135, 192
Earnings, of CLOs, 204
Eaton Vance Tax Advantaged Global
    Dividend (ETO), 124
Eaton Vance Tax Advantaged Global
    Dividend Opportunities (ETG), 124

Economic value:
  cash distributions as, 25
  of factories, 4
  of portfolios, 19
  stock value vs., 7
Efficient market hypothesis, 209
Einstein, Albert, 5
El-Erian, Mohamed, 115
Ellis, Charles, 5, 210
Emotional advantage:
  of aggressive and moderate strategies,
     117–118
  of Income Factory, 30–31, 56–57,
     140–141
  of Income Factory Light, 141
  of Income Factory strategy, 11
Energy and MLP funds, 98t, 101,
  135–136
Equity funds, 82, 98t–99t, 99
Equity indexing, 207
Equity investing strategies, 27
Equity investments:
  in collateralized loan obligations, 192
  risks with, 158–159
Equity returns, 33, 193–195
Equity risk, 76–77, 159, 161t
Equity-covered call funds, 98t, 102–103
ERC (Wells Fargo Multi-Sector Income),
  96
ETG (Eaton Vance Tax Advantaged
  Global Dividend Opportunities), 124
ETO (Eaton Vance Tax Advantaged
  Global Dividend), 124
Exchange-traded funds (ETFs), 156, 157
Exchange-traded notes (ETNs), 156, 157

FGB (First Trust Specialty Finance),
  101–102, 111, 123
Finance and banking funds, 98t,
  101–102
Financial goals, 65–67
First Trust Specialty Finance (FGB),
  101–102, 111, 123
Fixed income:
  portfolio growth from, 7
  risk/reward profile of, 154–157,
     174–175

Fixed income assets, 83, 92t–93t
FOF (Cohen & Steers Closed End
  Opportunity), 96, 122
Ford Motor, 3–4, 44
401k plans, 21–22
Fund types, 13, 87–105
  assembling portfolio with, 104–105
  convertible bonds, 97
  energy and MLP, 101
  equity-covered call, 102–103
  finance and banking, 101–102
  general equity, 103–104
  high-yield bonds, 94–95
  multi-asset funds, 96
  preferred, 96–97
  real estate, 99–100
  senior loans, 93–94
  utility/infrastructure, 100–101
Fundamental analysis, 209

GAAP accounting, 199
Gabelli Convertible & Income (GCV),
  123
Gabelli Global Utility & Income (GLU),
  100
General equity funds, 99t, 103–104
Graham, Benjamin, 24, 208, 209
Gross, Bill, 115
Growth companies, 27
Growth gaps, in investment strategies, 3
Growth portfolio, 44–46
Growth stocks:
  growth portfolio vs., 44–46
  as unnecessary in Income Factory
     strategy, 46–48
Growth-oriented model portfolio, 48,
  49t, 50

Harrison William Henry, 22
Heroic investing, 6
High-yield bond funds, 92t, 94–95
  as fixed income, 156
  risk/reward profile of, 164
  risks of, 172–174
High-yield corporate bonds, 166
High-yield credit, 172–174
High-yield debt, 130

High-yield investments:
  with fixed income, 155–157
  in Income Factory strategy, 60
  and risk, 78–79, 128–129
HYB (New America High Income), 95,
  120
Hyperinflationary economies, 160
HYT (Black Rock Corporate Hight
  Yield), 120

IFL (*see* Income Factory Light (IFL))
IGA (Voya Global Advantage &
  Opportunity), 123
IGR (CBRE Clarion Global Real Estate),
  122
Income, 19–28
  and changes in retirement plans, 21–22
  and collateralized loan obligations,
    188–192
  fixed, 7
  as focus of investment strategy, 1–2
  growth of, as benchmark, 25
  as historical focus of wealth, 20–21
  as purpose of investing, 10–11
  for retail vs. professional investors,
    22–28
  in turbulent stock market, 40
  yield and growth of, 126–128, 127*t*
Income Factory, 43–61
  as alternative to traditional investment
    strategies, 30–31, 47–48
  benefits of, 12, 56–57
  in current portfolio, 55–59
  evaluating appropriateness of, 64–65
  flexibility in, 73
  growth portfolio vs. growth stocks,
    44–46
  growth stocks as unnecessary in,
    46–48
  and Income Factory Light, 59–60
  investment strategies used in, 27
  maintaining, 16–17
  and personal attitude, 60–61
  portfolio examples of, 48–53
  resistance to, 11
  risks in, 54–55
  and stock market changes, 4–5

Income Factory Light (IFL), 12, 59–60,
  139–145
  aggressive investing in, 113
  dividend growth stock for, 141–142,
    142*t*
  investment selection for, 84–86, 86*t*
  models for, 143–145
  reasons for using, 140–142
  for taxable accounts, 149–151, 150*t*
Indexing, 210
Individual company risk, 78
Individual retirement accounts (IRAs),
  21–22, 79–80, 80*t*, 101, 145
Inflation, 168
Interest rate risk, 114–115, 159, 161*t*,
  166–169, 173–174
Investment managers, 72, 103
Investment philosophies, 15–16, 207–211
Investment selection, 63–86
  asset classes in, 82–86
  financial goals and timing in, 65–67
  for Income Factory Light, 60
  personal attitudes in, 67–69
  risk tolerance in, 69–73
  risk types in, 73–79
  tax considerations in, 79–82
Investment strategies:
  and age of investors, 65
  based on age of investors, 47
  based on market value, 31–32
  challenges facing, 38–39
  Income Factory strategy as alternative
    to, 30–31
  for short-term investments, 66–67
  used in Income Factory strategy, 27
  (*See also* Long-term investment
    strategy)
Investment style, 69–70
Investor sentiment, 70
Investors:
  age and appropriate strategies for, 47,
    65
  aggressive, 67–68
  attention to market value by, 68
IRAs (*see* Individual retirement accounts
  (IRAs))
ISE High Income™, 96

JMLP (Nuveen All Cap Energy MLP
    Opportunity), 123
John Hancock Financial Opportunities
    (BTO), 102, 123
JRI (Nuveen Real Asset Income &
    Growth), 122
JSD (Nuveen Short Duration Credit
    Opps), 120
Junk bonds, 95, 122, 157, 164, 178

Kelly, Walt, 22
KKR Income Opportunities (KIO), 95

LDP (Cohen & Steers Limited Duration
    Preferred & Income Fund), 122
Lee, James B., Jr., 215
Leverage:
    in closed-end funds, 131
    in collateralized loan obligations,
        188–189
    and fixed income, 156
    in general equity funds, 103–104
Liabilities:
    of banks, 196–197
    for collateralized loan obligations,
        190–192, 190t
Liquidity risk, 73–74, 78
London InterBank Offered Rate
    (LIBOR), 185
Long-term investment strategy:
    diversification in, 91
    Income Factory as, 4, 88–89
    market value in, 39–41
    real estate funds in, 99–100
    return rates and growth in, 35–36
Losses:
    default vs., 179–180
    on defaulted bonds and loans, 93–94
    paper, 55

Macquarie Global Infrastructure
    (MGU), 100
Macquarie/First Trust Global
    Infrastructure (MFD), 100
Malkiel, Burton, 209
Market downturns, 55
Market price risk, 78

Market value, 29–41
    as benchmark, 23–24
    and business performance, 32
    of collateralized loan obligations, 204
    as complex process, 36–39
    corporate actions affecting, 36–37
    dividend growth and stock price
        growth, 33–36
    as element of total return, 31–32
    of factories, 4
    importance of, for professional
        investors, 23
    income stream vs., 2
    in long-term investment strategy,
        39–41
    media attention to, 22–23, 31, 68
    portfolio growth through, 11
    as theoretical, 3
    traditional investment strategy based
        on, 31–32
Master limited partnerships (MLPs):
    complexity risk of, 76
    in energy and MLP funds, 101
    as fixed income, 156
    higher yield as typical in, 130
    in taxable accounts, 82
Mature companies, 27
MCI (Barings Corporate Investors), 95
Media attention, to market value, 22–23,
    31, 68
MFD (Macquarie/First Trust Global
    Infrastructure), 100
MGU (Macquarie Global Infrastructure),
    100
Model portfolios, 13, 107–124
    aggressive risk/reward profile—12
        funds, 109–111
    aggressive risk/reward profile—20
        funds, 112–113
    defining aggressive for, 113–118
    for Income Factory, 52, 53t
    moderate risk/reward profile—12
        funds, 118–119
    moderate risk/reward profile—24
        funds, 120–124
    taxable account, 148t, 149
    updates and revisions to, 16, 17

Moderate risk/reward profile—12 funds, 118–119, 119*t*

Moderate risk/reward profile—24 funds, 120–124, 121*t*

Mr. Darcy (character), 20

Multi-asset funds, 93*t*, 96

Mutual funds:
 closed-end funds vs., 130
 as diversification, 71

National Association of Insurance Commissioners, 214

New America High Income (HYB), 95, 120

New normal (term), 115

Nonheroic investing, 6

Non-investment grade companies, 94, 112, 157, 164, 177

Nuveen All Cap Energy MLP Opportunity (JMLP), 123

Nuveen Real Asset Income & Growth (JRI), 122

Nuveen Short Duration Credit Opps (JSD), 120

OFS Credit Company (OCCI), 192

Oxford Lane Capital (OXLC), 134–135, 192

Paper losses, 55

Paper profit, 24

Pass-through vehicles, 101

PCI (PIMCO Dynamic Credit Income), 95

P/E (price/earnings) ratio, 36–37

Perry, Oliver, 22*

Personal attitude:
 about investing decisions, 109
 and Income Factory strategy, 60–61
 in investment selection, 67–69
 and risk/reward profile, 111, 136–137

PIMCO Dynamic Credit Income (PCI), 95

Pogo (character), 22

Portfolio(s):
 assembling, 104–105
 economic and market values of, 26–27

examples of Income Factory strategy in, 48–53

Income Factory strategy in current, 55–59

Prairie Home Companion, 6

Preferred funds, 93*t*, 96–97

Preferred stock, 97, 156

Preferred stocks, 162

Price/earnings (P/E) ratio, 36–37

Principle risk, 78

Private placement conference, 214–215

Professional investors, 22–28

Psychological advantage:
 of aggressive and moderate strategies, 117–118
 of Income Factory, 56–57, 140–141
 of Income Factory Light, 141

RA (Brookfield Real Assets), 96

A Random Walk Down Wall Street (Malkiel), 209

Random walks, 210

Rational markets, 33–34

Real estate funds, 82, 98*t*, 99–100

Recovery, after default, 179–182

Recovery ratings, 182, 216–217

Reeves Utility Income (UTG), 100–102

Reinvestment:
 and diversification, 91
 growth provided by, 2, 44–45
 during market downturns, 55
 and portfolio growth, 26
 ramping down, 65–67
 Rule of 72 for, 35–36
 in tax-advantaged vs. taxable accounts, 80–82

Research:
 on collateralized loan obligations, 203–205
 on senior loans, 94
 on suitability of investments, 89

Resetting, of CLOs, 202–203

Retail investors, 22–28

Retirement plans:
 changes in, 21–22
 Income Factory strategy for, 65–66

Return(s):
   of Income Factory and traditional
      portfolios, 46–47
   from Income Factory strategy, 30, 43
   on senior loans, 185–186
   in traditional investment portfolios, 3
Return of capital (ROC):
   in collateralized loan obligations, 198,
      200–202, 204
   and tax advantaged funds, 147–148
   in taxable accounts, 82
Right things, doing, 5, 210
Risk(s):
   and aggressive portfolios, 114
   of debt instruments, 166–167
   familiar vs. unfamiliar, 157
   identifying acceptable, 77–79
   for Income Factory strategies, 12
   in Income Factory strategy, 54–55,
      70–71
   of Income Factory strategy, 40–41, 45
   in Income Factory strategy vs.
      traditional investment strategies,
      32
   layers of, 160–161, 161t
   of stockholders, 14
   for traditional investment strategies,
      12
   of traditional investment strategies,
      45, 54–55
   types of, 73–79
   and yield, 73, 128–129
Risk free, 161t, 168
Risk tolerance, 69–73
Risk/reward profile, 153–164, 185f
   of different asset classes, 157–161
   of fixed income, 154–157
   in Income Factory Light models,
      143–145
   and Rule of 72, 36
   of stocks, 161–164
ROC (see Return of capital (ROC))
Roth IRAs, 79, 145
Rule of 72, 35–36, 57–58, 80

Safety, of CLOs, 198–200
Scrooge McDuck (character), 21

Secured loans, 183–184
Secured Overnight Financing Rate
   (SOFR), 185*
Security, during market turbulence, 5
Security Analysis (Graham and Dodd),
   24, 209
Seeking Alpha blog site, 10, 17
Seeking Alpha website, 11, 27
Senior loans, 14, 92t, 93–94, 177–186
   as asset class, 180–182
   and collateralized loan obligations,
      188
   and credit loss, 184
   default vs. loss, 179–180
   returns on, 185–186
   stability of, 185–186
   two-dimensional credit modeling for,
      182–185
Short-term investments, 66–67
Siegel, Jeremy, 210–211
SOFR (Secured Overnight Financing
   Rate), 185*
S&P (Standard & Poor's), 214–217
Specialized asset classes, 72
Specialized vehicles, 130, 156, 157
Standard & Poor's (S&P), 214–217
Stock market:
   analytical methods applied to, 24
   changes in, and Income Factory
      investment strategy, 4–5
   changes in, and Income Factory
      strategy, 26
   downturns of, as opportunity for
      reinvestment, 55
   long-term performance of, 39–40
   security during turbulence in, 5
Stock price growth, 33–36
Stock value, 7
Stockholders:
   and equity risk, 77
   risk assumed by, 161–164
Stocks:
   corporate buybacks of, 38
   credit risk for, 174
   risk/reward profile of, 158, 161–164,
      174–175
   risks of, 14